# Cognitive-Behavioural Thera
# in the Treatment of Additio

# Cognitive-Behavioural Therapy in the Treatment of Addiction

## A Treatment Planner for Clinicians

**Christos Kouimtsidis**
*St. George's University of London*

**Martina Reynolds**
*Brunel University*

**Colin Drummond**
*St. George's University of London*

**Paul Davis**
*Camden and Islington Mental Health and Social Care Trust*

and

**Nicholas Tarrier**
*University of Manchester*

John Wiley & Sons, Ltd

Telephone (+44) 1243 779777

Email (for orders and customer service enquiries): cs-books@wiley.co.uk
Visit our Home Page on www.wiley.com



**Other Wiley Editorial Offices**

John Wiley & Sons Inc., 111 River Street, Hoboken, NJ 07030, USA

Jossey-Bass, 989 Market Street, San Francisco, CA 94103-1741, USA

Wiley-VCH Verlag GmbH, Boschstr. 12, D-69469 Weinheim, Germany

John Wiley & Sons Australia Ltd, 42 McDougall Street, Milton, Queensland 4064, Australia

John Wiley & Sons (Asia) Pte Ltd, 2 Clementi Loop #02-01, Jin Xing Distripark, Singapore 129809

John Wily & Sons Canada Ltd, 6045 Freemont Blvd, Mississauga, ONT, L5R 4J3, Canada

Wiley also publishes its books in a variety of electronic formats. Some content that appears in print may not be available in electronic books.

Anniversary Logo Design: Richard J. Pacifico

**Library of Congress Cataloging-in-Publication Data**

Cognitive-behavioural therapy in the treatment of addiction : a treatment planner for clinicians/Christos Kouimtsidis ... [et al.].
p. ; cm.
Includes bibliographical references and index.
ISBN 978-0-470-05852-7 (pbk. : alk. paper)
1. Substance abuse–Treatment. 2. Cognitive therapy. I. Kouimtsidis, Christos.
[DNLM: 1. Substance-Related Disorders–therapy. 2. Cognitive Therapy.
3. Patient Care Planning. WM 270 C6764 2007]
RC564.C6225 2007
616.86'06–dc22

2007017037

**British Library Cataloguing in Publication Data**

A catalogue record for this book is available from the British Library

ISBN 978-0-470-05852-7 (pbk)

Typeset in 10/13pt Scala and Scala Sans by Thomson Digital, India
Printed and bound in Great Britain by Antony Rowe Ltd, Chippenham, Wiltshire
This book is printed on acid-free paper responsibly manufactured from sustainable forestry in which at least two trees are planted for each one used for paper production.

# Contents

# About the Authors

**Christos Kouimtsidis**, MBBS, MSc, MRCPsych, is Consultant Psychiatrist at NW Herts Community Drug and Alcohol Team, Hertfordshire Partnership NHS Trust and Honorary Senior Lecturer at Section of Addictive Behaviour, St George's, University of London since 2003. He was Specialist Registrar and later Clinical Lecturer in Addiction Psychiatry at St George's from 1998. His MSc dissertation in 1996 was on CBT in substance misuse. His doctorate is an investigation of the role of expectancies and schemas in treatment and relapse of substance misuse. He has been involved in quantitative and qualitative research including epidemiology research in general hospital, co-morbidity and psychological approaches in addiction, staff and services users' experiences of treatment provision. He is a tutor for the postgraduate courses at St George's, and he has also led a number of seminars and workshops on CBT in substance misuse. His clinical team provides services for drugs and alcohol in a large geographical area in Hertfordshire consisting of small urban and rural settlements.

**Martina Reynolds**, MA, PhD, is a Senior Lecturer at the School of Social Sciences of Brunel University. Prior to this she was research lecturer in Addiction at St George's, University of London, where she developed her interest in the topic. She obtained her BA/MA in Psychology from the University of Oxford and her PhD from the University of London. She has extensive research experience and has published in the fields of substance use, trauma, post-traumatic stress disorders and depression. She has also convened and taught both undergraduate and postgraduate modules on addiction and related areas.

**Colin Drummond**, MBChB, MD, FRCPsych, is Professor of Addiction Psychiatry and Consultant Psychiatrist at St George's Hospital Medical School and South West London and Head of Addiction Behaviour at St George's NHS Trust, where he has been since 1993. Before that he was Lecturer and later Senior Lecturer in Addiction Behaviour at the Medical Research Council Addiction Research Unit, National Addiction Centre, Institute of Psychiatry from 1987. His doctorate was on the subject of alcohol and public health. He is Principal Investigator on several research grants including the Department of Health funded national alcohol needs assessment project and a new national research programme on screening and brief alcohol intervention, also funded by the Department of Health. Professor Drummond is also Assistant Editor of the journal *Addiction*. He has published papers on a wide range of topics including epidemiology, clinical trials, drug and alcohol policy and theories of craving. He leads the alcohol treatment service in South West London providing inpatient and community-based interventions. He has been closely involved in providing advice to government on alcohol and drug misuse strategy. He is a member of the Models of Care working group which has produced a national framework for drug and alcohol services in England. He is a member of the Faculty of Substance Misuse of the Royal College of Psychiatrists and served as the Academic Secretary. He is also the Director of the Specialist Clinical Addiction Network based at the National Treatment Agency. He is a member of the American Psychiatric Association/World Health Organization Substance Use Disorders Working Group on the fifth revision of the *Diagnostic and Statistical Manual*. He is also a member of the WHO Expert Committee on Drug Dependence and Alcohol Problems.

**Paul Davis** has worked in the NHS for over 30 years, the majority of which has been as a specialist clinician in alcohol and drug work. He is Consultant Clinical Psychologist and Honorary Senior Lecturer at University College London, and Camden and Islington Mental Health and Social Care Trust, London, where he is also Head of Substance Misuse Psychology Services. His clinical interests include the practice and development of cognitive and behavioural therapies with complex cases, and psychological assessment and management of patients with a dual diagnosis. His main areas of research have focused on evaluating the efficacy and effectiveness of NHS interventions in clinical settings, outcome monitoring, prevention outcome evaluation, forensic aspects of drug abuse and neuropsychological changes in people with drug addiction. Dr Davis is a practitioner and trainer in CBT and he has presented over 100 invited workshops in CBT and motivational interviewing (MI) applied in the field of substance misuse. He provides supervision and consultation in MI and CBT to health professionals from a number of NHS Trusts. He has co-authored and contributed to treatment research manuals in this field and has conducted treatment outcome trials on psychological interventions with problem drug and alcohol users. Dr Davis has served on the British Psychological Society Faculty of Addiction Committee for over 10 years and was Chair for several years. He is a National Assessor for Consultant Psychology posts in the NHS and has served on numerous national committees on substance misuse, most recently on the National Institute for Health and Clinical Excellence Guidance Development Groups in substance misuse.

**Nicholas Tarrier** is Professor of Clinical Psychology, Head of the Division of Clinical Psychology and Research Director of the School of Psychological Sciences, University of Manchester, UK, and Honorary Consultant Clinical Psychologist in the Manchester Mental Health and Social Care NHS Trust. He has held academic posts at universities in Brazil and Australia. He has a long-standing interest in the practice and evaluation of Cognitive-Behaviour Therapy and its application to a wide range of disorders.

# Foreword

Cognitive-behavioural therapy (CBT) has emerged as the leading evidence-based practice in the treatment of psychological disorders, including both interventions for mental health and addictive behaviour problems. The authors of this book are to be commended for providing therapists with a comprehensive manual outlining CBT principles and practices in the treatment of addiction. They have successfully integrated intervention strategies derived from the theoretical models based on cognitive psychology, social learning theory, and behaviour change principles. Major treatment approaches based on these theoretical approaches are described in detail by the authors, including cognitive therapy, motivational interviewing, and relapse prevention. Both experienced therapists and those in training will benefit from reading this most recent book on CBT in the treatment of addiction.

Readers are provided with an overview of CBT as it is applied in a structured treatment programme. Unlike other approaches to addiction treatment, CBT adopts a client-centered orientation, based on mutual collaboration between therapist and client as they work together to help resolve the presenting problem. This is in sharp distinction to other intervention strategies, including those derived from the moral model of addiction (clients must be confronted in an authoritative 'top-down' approach in which they are prescribed specific treatment goals). CBT is an individualized treatment approach, in which each client is considered to be a unique case, with different risk factors and coping skills. The focus on matching treatment strategies to each client's individual needs is very different from the traditional medical model in which addiction is defined as a disease, and that treatment must follow the same pharmaceutical prescriptions and/or the same Twelve-Step Path to recovery. In CBT, clients learn that there are multiple pathways for successful behaviour change, and that the therapist will help them find the way that works best for them. The client's goal is to move forward in finding the right path to change, and the therapist is there to provide a 'toolbox' of clinical techniques to help the client arrive at their chosen destination. As such, the treatment process over time could be considered more a journey of personal 'discovery', not just one focused on 'recovery'.

There are many positive features to this treatment manual. Each clinical technique is presented in a definitive manner, including a description and overview of its treatment implications, and a discussion of how to apply the technique, including case examples. A wide range of both behavioural and cognitive strategies is included. Therapists will appreciate the attention given to agenda setting and how to structure each therapy session as treatment proceeds. Clinical assessment (including functional analysis of the addictive behaviour) is also covered, along with an excellent discussion of how to proceed with case formulation. The topic of therapist training and supervision is also included. One of the best features of this book is that it includes a thorough description of treatment approaches for clients with co-occurring disorders in the 'elective topics' chapter. Given that so many of our clients come to treatment with a dual diagnosis (e.g., depression and alcohol dependence), therapists need to provide them with an integrated treatment approach to help them cope with both problems (e.g., learning more adaptive ways of coping with depression instead of drinking in an attempt to self-medicate their symptoms). Given that CBT has been shown to be effective in the treatment of both mental health problems and addictive behaviours, clients will benefit from working with therapists who are experienced in both domains.

In conclusion, I salute the authors for putting together their clinical expertise in developing this CBT manual. It would be incorrect to describe the present volume as a treatment 'cook-book' in which therapists are told what to do in a rigid step-by-step manner. Rather, the authors have provided therapists with a manual of menus, with different ingredients and alternative preparation methods that can be helpful in serving up an effective CBT programme to satisfy each and every client's appetite for change. Enjoy the feast!

G. Alan Marlatt, Ph.D.,
Professor of Psychology,
Director, Addictive Behaviors Research Center,
University of Washington.

# Preface

Addiction is a complex phenomenon with a number of associated parameters and ways of addressing it. As a phenomenon or human behaviour it has been documented in various forms going back to the ancient civilizations of Greece and Rome and before. It is therefore no surprise that there is a major interest in it from sociological, anthropological, philosophical and clinical perspectives with some conflicting and complementary views expressed.

As a clinician working in the field of addiction, one is faced with and must consider all aspects of the phenomenon, however, it is also necessary to focus on one's duty as a clinician: to help individuals who seek help to modify their addictive behaviour with the most effective and appropriate means available. In everyday clinical practice there is usually little that one can do about society's attitude, resources available for treatment and recovery or rehabilitation, governmental choices or funding allocation. What one is faced with as a clinician is to work within the treatment system limitations to help the individual and the family.

Therefore it is important to understand the individual as a person and see beyond the addiction problem without at the same time losing clinical focus. To this effect one needs to have a theoretical framework which is flexible and adaptable, but structured. A theoretical model that puts the individual in the centre; that can be shared with the individual and the family, and that is linked with a specific and structured therapy tool.

Cognitive-behavioural therapy can be such a tool. In this book we share our experience of using CBT to help individuals with addiction problems, and we hope that the book will be helpful as an everyday tool for fellow clinicians.

# Acknowledgements

The authors would like to thank the following mental health workers, who agreed to take part in the UKCBTMM trial and to use the CBT manual developed for the trial, the precursor of this book:

Mr. Kevin Darbyshire, Mr Terry Orr, Dr Dominic O'Ryan, Dr Liz McGrath, (Camden and Islington Substance Misuse Service- North London); Dr Doug Handyside, Ms Kate Weeks, Mr Jonathan West, (Brighton Substance Misuse Service); Ms Carol Houghton, Ms Vicki Obi, (Manchester Drug Service); Ms Linda Kelly, Ms Jane Wilcock, Ms Jane Wolfendale, (Salford Drug Service); Ms Coral Harvey, Dr Rebecca Lee, Ms Pam Lievesley, (Drugs North West, Prestwich, Manchester; NB: not a study site); Dr Bethany O'Connell, Ms Hina Rahimi, Mr Phillipe Rahman, Mr Raj Seegobin, Mr Karl Williams, (South London and St George's Mental Health NHS Trust Drug Service- South London); Ms Debbie Wilkinson, Mr Tim Bennett, (Bolton Substance Misuse Service); Ms Nicky Armitage, Ms Cath Harbridge, Ms Lucy Harrison, Mr John Parr, (Wigan and Leigh Substance Misuse Service); Ms Sue Harris, Mr Paul MacGregor, Ms Shamiso Mubwandarika, Ms Carolyne Savage, (Liverpool Substance Misuse Service).

We would also like to thank Dr. Louise Sell and Dr. Douglas Turkington for their contribution in the development of the UKCBTMM trial CBT manual. We would also like to thank Dr. Abigail Rose and Katherine Perryman for their contribution to the literature review.

# CHAPTER ONE

# Overview and use of the book



## Who was this book written for?

This book has been written for clinicians working in the field of substance misuse. It will also be useful to other professional groups such as clinicians in mental health, staff in general health services, and students of psychology, counselling and related disciplines.

1. In the UK, staff working in the substance misuse field come from a range of professional backgrounds and expertise as far as psychosocial interventions for substance misuse are concerned. Depending on the nature of the role (professional background and setting), staff might find themselves using psychotherapeutic approaches as a primary intervention, alternatively, psychotherapeutic intervention may be used in conjunction with other interventions. Today, the majority of clinicians and other health care professionals working within substance misuse services have some understanding of cognitive-behaviour theory and its application in the field, and have some training in related therapeutic models, for example motivational interviewing.

This book will facilitate theoretical understanding of cognitive theory, but for the most part, it is a handbook for use in everyday clinical practice. Basic training or knowledge of cognitive-behaviour therapy (CBT) in the treatment of substance use although not necessary, will enhance the potential of the clinical use of the book. Regular supervision by a professional trained in the application of CBT (preferably with experience in substance misuse) is crucial.

2. For clinicians who are trained and have experience in the application of psychological interventions, particularly cognitive-behavioural interventions, but have limited experience in the treatment of substance misuse, this book will bridge that gap. It provides a model and treatment planner of how to work with individuals with either a primary substance misuse problem or co-morbidity (mental health and substance misuse) using cognitive-behavioural approaches applied to substance misuse.
3. Health service staff (primary or secondary, community or inpatient) treat people with substance misuse problems. Such problems might not be the presenting

condition/problem, but might influence overall treatment progress. The book will facilitate the acquisition of a more comprehensive psychological understanding of addictions and skills to work with such clients, within the treatment setting in which they work.

4. Whilst this book does not claim to be a comprehensive textbook on the subject, it can be used as a practical guide and in conjunction with other CBT texts. In this sense, it can be used as a training tool for psychology students, psychiatrists, counsellors and therapists.

In this book, the term 'substance misuse' includes alcohol misuse, whereas the term 'drugs' refers to illicit substances. The terms 'misuse' and 'abuse' are used interchangeably. The term client is used instead of patient as it is more widely accepted across professionals in the field.

## ▶ Sources and development of the book

This book was developed from the treatment manual used in the UKCBTMM study (United Kingdom Cognitive-Behaviour Therapy study in Methadone Maintenance treatment), funded by the Department of Health Substance Use Initiative from 2000 to 2004. This was a pragmatic study of the effectiveness and cost effectiveness of CBT as an adjunct to regular keyworking of methadone substitution treatment for opioid dependence. Staff from services across the UK (nurses, social workers, psychiatrists and psychologists), with minimum or no training in CBT in substance misuse settings were trained and accredited on the theory and application of CBT delivered according to the manual. They also received regular supervision provided by CBT-trained clinical psychologists or psychiatrists. All sessions were tape-recorded. Adherence to the protocol and quality of CBT was monitored using appropriate instruments.

The model presented in this book is not new in the sense that it does not propose new concepts. It does attempt to bring together two different cognitive-behavioural applications: the relapse prevention and skills training models based on social learning theory; and Beck's cognitive model based upon his earlier models of depression and anxiety. As will be become apparent, these models have a lot in common, but they differ as far as structure, focus and emphasis is concerned (Figure 1.1).

## ▶ How to use the book

This book is designed to provide a structured programme, which can be adapted to the needs of individual clients. The overall programme, the topics covered and session structure, is standard and should be closely adhered to. However, the time devoted to particular topics (number of sessions) and techniques used can be varied and adapted to the needs of individuals. An outline of what is covered in each chapter of the book is described below.

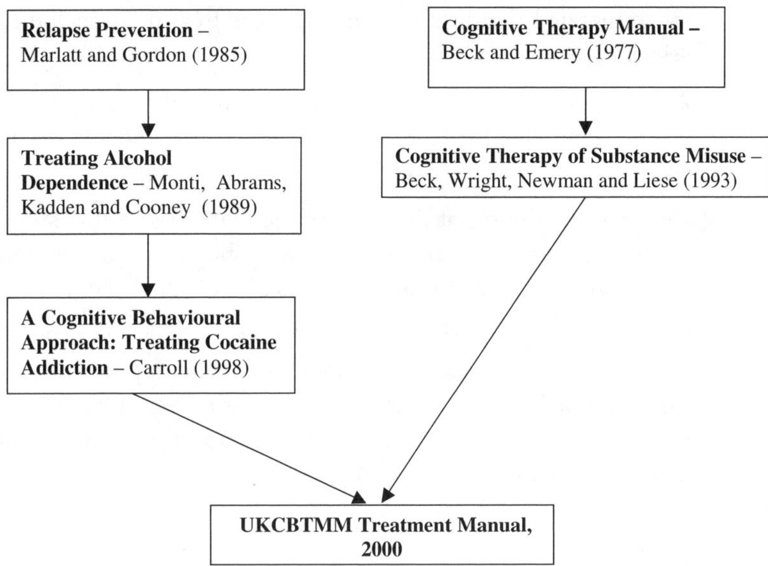


**Figure 1.1** Development of this CBT model.

### *Part I*

- General overview of cognitive-behaviour therapy, the cognitive model of addiction and review of the current research evidence.
- Description of cognitive and behavioural techniques used in therapy. Each technique will be described generally under the following headings: definition, case example, when it should be used (topics/problems for which the technique might be used), and problems (types of problems/things that go wrong and solutions to put them right). Topics are divided into 'core topics' (e.g. dealing with stimulus conditions, problem solving) which apply to most clients with substance abuse problems, and 'elective topics' (such as depression and compulsive criminal behaviour) which only apply to certain clients. The selection of elective topics is based upon the formulation of the individual client's problem at the beginning of treatment. However, as the formulation can be adapted and changed through treatment, these may change. The therapist may use a variety of techniques in one topic, or adhere to a few specific techniques as required. Although techniques are recommended for use in different topics, these are only recommendations, and the technique/intervention used should be the one that works best for the client. This may mean that in practice a number of different techniques are tried.

### *Part II*

- A detailed description of the session structure, time allocation and length of treatment. The discussion about session structure is relevant to all sessions and topics (core and elective) covered in the treatment programme, and it is recommended that it is used through the treatment, including the assessment sessions.

- A description of the assessment (functional analysis and case formulation). This will form the basis for decisions about which topics should be covered in the future sessions.
- Detailed description of the core topics, that is those that should be included in the treatment programme for all clients. The number of sessions devoted to each topic may be adapted to suit the needs of individual clients.
- Outline description of the elective topics and advice on how to use the topics presented. Only topics relevant to the individual's problems should be included. They may be included at various points in the overall treatment programme. The overall structure of the session is the same as for the core topics, and the techniques can be adapted to these problems.

### *Part III*

- Therapist training and supervision. This section details appropriate methods to train and supervise clinicians working in CBT in the substance misuse field.

Part I is an extensive introduction to the theory and principles of cognitive-behaviour theory and practice. It is particularly important for those who are not familiar with the principles of the theory. It also provides guidance on cognitive and behavioural techniques most relevant in the field of substance misuse. We consider that it is necessary to have a separate chapter on the cognitive and behavioural techniques, in order to enable clinicians to understand, practice and become familiar with them and use them appropriately in treatment sessions in different clinical settings (whether as part of a structured therapy approach or not).

Part II is the core of the book. Therapists experienced in the use of CBT in general can skip Part I and focus on this section of the book. The aim is to be explicit, practical and descriptive so that those without CBT experience can use it in everyday clinical practice as an aid when preparing for a session or even during the session. More experienced staff can be more flexible on how to structure sessions and what to include. CBT is a collaborative approach. Both client and therapist bring to the treatment their unique experiences and skills, and they work together to facilitate the client to take control of decisions, and raise awareness and potential for alternatives both in relation to substance use and lifestyle in general. Treatment should therefore be flexible and open to change so that individual goals can be accommodated. Part II is a description of how to apply CBT principles that enhance collaboration and put the client in the centre of treatment process, whilst at the same time providing a general blueprint of what to do step by step.

Part III addresses training and supervision. This section refers to our experience from the UKCBTMM trial as well as previously gained experience. It also provides useful tools/worksheets for between-session practice which is very important for a successful outcome.

## Addictions addressed in this book

The earlier CBT models were developed for the treatment of one substance of abuse, and later modified and tested with others (Beck and Emery, 1977; Beck *et al.*, 1993; Marlatt and Gordon, 1985; Monti *et al.*, 1989; Carroll, 1998). This suggests that the principles of CBT in addiction are common across substances and models, and may be used successfully for the treatment of different substance misuse problems, in different treatment settings, with the appropriate modifications. The model presented in this book may also be applied to different substances of abuse.

This book does not address nicotine addiction and gambling. Although the model could be applied to such addictions, clinical interventions and research relating to these conditions has been developed separately from what are traditionally known as services and research for treatment of substance misuse. A distinctive group of clients are those misusing medication for pain control. Currently in the UK, treatment for such clients is not the remit of specialist substance misuse services (tier 3 services, Models of Care, NTA, 2002). They are treated in primary care with the support of community pain specialist teams (Pain Society, 2004). However, we consider that the model described in this book could be used for the treatment of this client group, and we will expand on necessary modifications required. A further client group that might be distinctive in their presentation and the relevant goal of the treatment intervention are those who present in general medical settings (i.e. medical or surgical wards) for problems related or not to their substance use. We will describe in some detail how aspects of the model can be used in nonspecialist settings.

CHAPTER TWO

# Introduction to cognitive-behaviour theory and research evidence



## Introduction to cognitive-behaviour therapy

Cognitive-behaviour therapy (CBT) has been established as one of the leading psychological interventions for mental health conditions. As the name implies, CBT has roots in both cognitive and behaviour therapies, but it is not simply a combination of cognitive and behavioural techniques. CBT is based on theoretical concepts and models that have been and continue to be the subject of extensive research and evaluation. Early cognitive-behavioural models of depression and panic disorder not only have empirical/clinical support, but have been further supported by outcome research studies. In the early days of theory and therapy development, major emphasis was given to separating the new approach from previous approaches (i.e. psychoanalytic), and to the unique characteristics of the new models. At a later stage, process research was employed to test the validity of concepts and their role in the development of mental health problems, as well as recovery from the same. Findings from process research, as well as ongoing research with either more complicated/pervasive conditions (such as eating disorders, personality disorders and psychotic disorders), or longer term follow-up studies incorporated modifications into or expanded some of the earlier models, and sometimes fused the boundaries with other theories or therapies (e.g. Fairburn Cooper and Shafran 1998, 2003). Other newer psychological approaches have been developed since, either based on similar theories or combining different theories. Some of them are based on empirical evidence and others on research findings. Nowadays, there are several cognitive-behavioural or related models targeted for the treatment of different disorders, all of which share some basic characteristics or theory principles.

The history of science proves that nothing has been developed in a vacuum. New ideas and theories are based on work inherited from previous generations. In this way, to understand cognitive-behavioural therapy it is necessary to review the principles of behavioural therapy (BT) as well as the principles of cognitive therapy (CT).

### *Behavioural theory and therapy*

Behaviourism was introduced to psychology by John Watson in 1913. Watson wanted to make psychology more scientific, and insisted that the focus of attention should be restricted to observable behaviour. He criticized Freud's approach, which relied upon introspection, case studies and constructs such as the unconscious which could not be measured. Behaviourists on the other hand adopted scientific assumptions, and regard behaviour as being determined by environmental influences.

Behaviour therapy is based upon two theories, which were developed at the beginning of the twentieth century: (a) classical conditioning and (b) operant conditioning, developed by Pavlov and Skinner, respectively.

**a.** According to Pavlov's classical conditioning model, a specific stimulus produces a known response. Conditioning is the process by which a previously unimportant or irrelevant stimulus becomes important or relevant, or in other words associated with an important behaviour. Pavlov used involuntary reflexes in his studies, that is behaviours that are not under voluntary control of the organism, and are generally associated with survival, for example salivation, blinking, coughing, and so on. In his classic experiment, food was the unconditioned stimulus (UCS – food produces the response), and salivation was the unconditioned response (UCR)

Food--------- > salivation
UCS------------ > UCR

Pavlov then used a bell as the neutral stimulus (NS) prior to the UCS.

Bell-----food------ > salivation
NS-------UCS------ > UCR

Eventually the bell alone resulted in salivation.

Bell--------- > salivation
CS------------ > CR

The neutral stimulus, became a conditioned stimulus (CS), which elicited a conditioned response (CR), salivation. This response is learned, and has been replicated using different species and different behaviours successfully, and is called 'classical conditioning' (Sue et al., 2003).

**b.** Operant conditioning was developed by Skinner. According to Skinner's model, the organism operates on its environment, and behaviour is modified by its consequences. The association between the response and the consequences is learned by the organism/subject, and the response is repeated with greater or lesser frequency depending on the type of consequence. The consequences are called reinforcement. There are two types of reinforcement: (i) primary reinforcement which is natural and satisfies basic drives, that is when we are hungry we eat, and eating stops hunger; and (ii) secondary/conditioned reinforcement where reinforcement can increase the frequency of a behaviour by: (a) enhancing or the addition of a pleasant experience (positive, e.g. 'when I work longer hours, I get paid extra'), or (b) removing or diminishing an unpleasant one (negative, e.g. 'when I feel stressed, alcohol relaxes me'). They can also reduce the frequency of a behaviour (punishing or aversion, e.g. 'if I shout in the cinema, I am escorted out'). Secondary reinforcement can help to maintain behaviour when primary reinforcements are not present (Sue *et al.*, 2003).

The application of the above models to explaining unwanted or challenging behaviours is explained as follows. So-called abnormal behaviour is a result of inappropriate conditioning that could be reshaped into so-called normal behaviour by using appropriate 'reinforcement contingencies'. Neurotic disorders were regarded as being the product of environmental events, but such learning processes were thought to have been influenced by inherited factors. Anxiety disorders were thought to be a result of unfortunate conditioning events, for example traumatic conditioning or repeated subtraumatic episodes. Systematic desensitization formed the basis of modern behavioural techniques used in the treatment of fear reduction and related anxiety. Some types of anxiety, however, persist in the absence of a fear-inducing stimulus. Mowrer (1960) attempted to explain this problem with a two-stage model of fear and avoidance. He argued that avoidance persisted because it successfully reduced fear or anxiety in the short term. Relief-inducing behaviour (avoidance) is strengthened and becomes the predominant behaviour to prevent exposure to the fear stimulus and as a result fear is maintained.

Hans Eysenck (1952)made behaviour therapy the leading form of psychotherapy, and he disputed the notion that neuroses were caused by unconscious conflicts, and that the symptoms were a defence against distress. Between 1970 and 1980, an era of research started in which the claims of therapeutic efficacy were tested and evaluated. The greatest progress was achieved with anxiety disorders, but progress in the treatment of depression, psychotic disorders and eating disorders was poor. BT was attractive to the scientific community because it was an approach that could be scientifically justified.

### *Cognitive theory and therapy*

Cognitive therapy (CT) was developed by Beck (1967, 1976). According to Beck, what is important for the individual is not the experience itself, but the meaning that the individual attaches to the experience, or in other words the interpretation of the experience by the individual. According to Beck there are three levels of beliefs or cognitive structures:

1. Schemas/schemata (or core beliefs), which are deep-rooted beliefs formed early in life as a result of early life experiences. Schemas affect an individual's view of himself, the world and the future. Because schemas are developed early in life, they are relatively stable structures (difficult to modify), but they can also influence the meaning that will be attributed to experiences later in life.

Examples of schemas: 'I am bad'; 'I don't deserve love'; 'life is unpredictable'; 'nobody can be trusted'.

2. Conditional beliefs are the result of the interaction between the individual and the environment, and important others. Conditional beliefs are based on schemas and they always have a behavioural component. They are the result of learning processes, and arise due to the repetition of certain experiences as a result of certain actions. They are expressed as 'if' statements.

   Example of conditional beliefs: 'If I do things perfectly, my parents will love me'.

3. Automatic thoughts are very superficial. They are brief thoughts or images and they come to mind suddenly. They are the first step of information processing and attribution of meaning to an event. Although they are brief and superficial they can have an influence on an individual's emotional state or behaviour. They are usually compatible with the individual's conditional beliefs and schemas, and they are prone to cognitive distortions. Examples of automatic thoughts: 'I can't do this'; 'this is bad'.

Perception and interpretation of events may be distorted due to cognitive processing errors. Common distortions include the following:

- *Overgeneralization*: this is making sweeping judgements on the basis of single instances. For example a person who made one mistake might conclude: 'I always do things wrong'; or a person who relapses into drug use following a period of abstinence concludes: 'I will never be strong'.
- *Selective abstraction*: this is attending only to negative aspects of experiences. For example, a person might state: 'this summer was awful, I didn't enjoy a single day of it', not because this is true, but because pleasurable memories failed to enter awareness.
- *Dichotomous thinking*: this means thinking in extremes or 'black and white thinking'. For example a person might ignore anything other than a perfect achievement: 'Unless I am the best, I am a failure', or 'there is no point in trying if I cannot be perfect for my family'.
- *Personalization*: this implies taking responsibility for things that have little or nothing to do with oneself. A client who arrives late for an appointment might think: 'there must be something wrong with me', ignoring the fact that there was a major road accident on the way to the clinic.
- *Arbitrary inference*: this means jumping to conclusions on the basis of inadequate evidence. For example a person who on his first day at work concludes: 'this job is not for me' (Fennell in Hawton *et al.*, 1995).

When cognitive distortions are applied to information, the individual is unable to appraise the information objectively. The result is the creation of distorted beliefs, which can influence feelings and behaviour. Such distorted beliefs can be present for a long time and can play a role in the development of mental disorders, and therefore become dysfunctional. In other words, dysfunctional beliefs are developed as a result of distortions in information processing, which may be affected by a number of factors including previous experience, mood and expectations.

As already mentioned, the central notion of cognitive therapy is that it is not the event(s), but the interpretation of event(s), and the meaning attached to this that gives rise to the problems that people experience. People experiment with and develop a range of ways of coping with the problems that they experience which can be both practical and emotional. Some work, some do not, and over time people come to rely on the ways that they feel work for them in certain situations. We strive for meaning in our lives, and to make sense of the sometimes unpredictable world we live in. Consistency is one way of making the unpredictable predictable. Therefore successful ways of coping with one problem can become patterns for dealing with others, and in that way stop the individual from finding new ways to face new challenges. The aim of treatment is not to teach people to think in the 'right' way according to social norms and values, but to enable them to consider alternative options, to make the decisions that they want to make, and to be responsible for them and their consequences.

### *Cognitive-behaviour therapy*

Cognitive-behaviour therapy (CBT) is based on both cognitive and behavioural theories and it is the product of introducing the study of internal mental processes and incorporating this element into behavioural theory following the scientific paradigm. New concepts have been defined, measured and validated. Cognitive-behaviour therapies share the same basic characteristics: they are all collaborative, structured, brief and focused.

- Collaborative means that the approach is client centred. Both client and therapist are important and need to share and agree on the aims of the treatment. Therapy is not something that is happening to the individual, but the individual is actively involved in the treatment process. The client's experience and interpretation is as important as therapist's, with the therapist being active in helping the client to consider alternative interpretations and possibilities. Practise of agreed activities and achievement of graded tasks is crucial for treatment progress.
- Structure is necessary in order to be collaborative, focused and in the 'here and now' when addressing the problems that the client presents. Structure doesn't exclude flexibility, and there is always space for revision and change of direction. Both client and therapist are responsible for setting and following the structure of the therapy.
- Most CBT models offer a specific number of sessions, usually based on theory and clinical evidence. For pervasive disorders such as eating disorders and personality disorders (as well as addiction), the models used are not open ended, and although the exact number of sessions might not be specified, it is not anticipated that it will be a long-term ongoing process.

- Treatment is focused and has as a starting point in the here and now. Although early experiences are important in the formation of schemas, and therefore may be the basis of current difficulties, the initial goal of therapy is not to change deep-rooted and stable structures.

Cognitive-behaviour therapy is not: (a) a simple 'pick and mix' exercise of cognitive and behaviour techniques, although some techniques can be used in isolation, outside the full model; (b) an education process, in which the wise therapist or group leader educates or enlightens clients on the truth or the right interpretation of life events, although education, clarification and enabling clients to define and understand experiences and feelings are important components of the therapy; (c) a cook book exercise or recipe for success where the relationship between the client and the therapist is not important, although treatment can be manual guided and the sessions structured; (d) easy or simplistic, it requires training and supervision in order to be effective, although training can be short and accessible to different people.

## Cognitive-behavioural therapy of substance use

As with other mental health conditions, several cognitive/cognitive-behavioural models of addiction have been developed. Whilst they do not all focus on exactly the same elements of the process of psychotherapy, there is some overlap, and sometimes different words are used to describe similar concepts. This chapter includes a description of the two most important models, followed by a description of a synthetic model proposed in this book.

### *Relapse prevention model (Marlatt and Gordon, 1985)*

Perhaps the most well-known model of addiction is Marlatt's relapse prevention model (Marlatt and Gordon, 1985). This model is based on Bandura's social learning theory (Bandura, 1977). It was developed for individuals abstinent from alcohol following residential treatment. It was also used and tested with other substances such as cigarettes, stimulants and opioids (more information on research will be given in the following section).

Bandura introduces the concept of self-efficacy, which is a perception or judgement of one's capability to execute a particular course of action required to deal effectively with an impending situation. Substance misuse is a socially acquired behaviour, which is influenced by several antecedent cues and re-enforcers. Between the stimulus and the response, some internal cognitive processes take place. Linked with social learning theory is expectancy theory, according to which there are two main factors that determine the initiation and repetition of a specific behaviour by a human being: outcome expectancy and efficacy expectancy. Outcome expectancy is the belief that a specific outcome will occur following a certain behaviour, for example by following a certain route you arrive at work on time. Efficacy expectation is the belief that you are able to execute the above behaviour, for example that you will be able to drive on a motorway. According to existing cognitive models of addiction, successful treatment is a result of a reduction in positive outcome expectancies and an increase in negative outcome expectancies, from use of the substance and as a result of the treatment respectively, and an increase in self-efficacy. Increased self-efficacy is thought to be the result of improved coping skills in response to situations linked with substance use.

According to the relapse prevention model, when an individual experiences a 'high-risk situation' (such as encountering cues, social pressure to drink, negative emotional states), the individual is more likely to relapse in the presence of high positive outcome expectancies and low self-efficacy. Positive outcome expectancy might be that drinking would effectively relieve a negative emotional state such as anxiety, or increase social confidence (e.g. 'I will feel better if I had a drink right now'). Self-efficacy (Bandura, 1977) is, in this context, the confidence that an individual has to resist the temptation to drink or use drugs. A further concept is the abstinence violation effect, in which individual's beliefs about the inevitability of being unable to control their drinking will encourage progression from an initial lapse to full reinstatement of use. Thus, within this model, the likelihood of relapse will depend on a complex interplay between these cognitive processes (Figure 2.1).

The Relapse Prevention model was originally developed for clients who had achieved abstinence, and the aim of treatment was to enable them to maintain their abstinence with a focused and practical treatment approach. Since then, the model (and the cognitive coping skills training model) has been used with clients still using substances with the aim of enabling them to gain control and make a decision not to use when faced with 'high-risk situations'.

Marlatt's model has been further developed by Niaura and colleagues to incorporate the role of cues, self-efficacy and conditioned craving in the relapse process (Niaura, 2000). In effect, high-risk situations, such as drug-paired stimuli or negative or positive affect increase urges to use drugs, which in turn, undermines self-efficacy, leading to drug use. Self-efficacy in this model is mediated by coping skills (an individual's ability to respond positively to a high-risk situation). In this

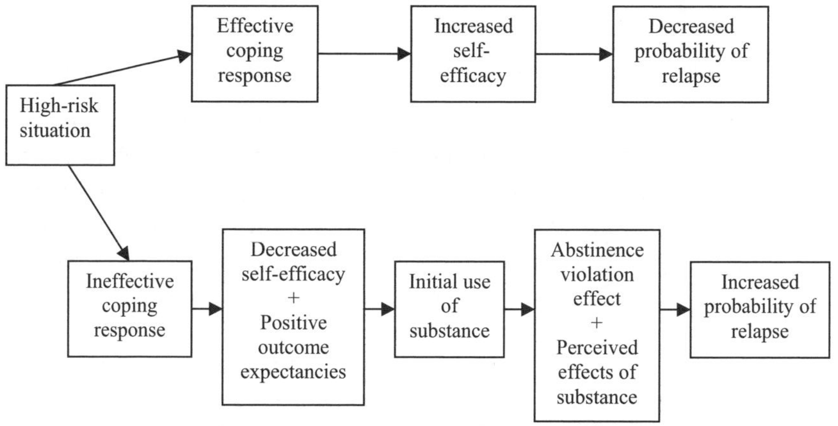


**Figure 2.1** Cognitive-behavioural model of relapse (Marlatt and Gordon, 1985).

model, importantly, coping skills can be developed within an appropriately tailored therapy.

Later Witkiewitz and Marlatt (2004) proposed a dynamic model of relapse to replace the earlier model. They proposed that there was a dynamic interaction between a number of factors leading to, and during, a high-risk situation. The individual faces the challenge of balancing multiple cues and possible consequences. The individual's response is described as an 'interactive system incorporating distal risk factors (e.g. family history, social support, co-morbid psychopathology), cognitive processes (e.g. self-efficacy, outcome expectancies, craving, abstinence violation effect, motivation) and cognitive and behavioural coping skills'. Situational cues (proximal risk factors) are considered still to play a prominent role between risk factors and substance use behaviour (Marlatt and Donovan, 2005).

### *Cognitive coping skills training (Monti et al., 1989)*

This model was developed for alcohol users following inpatient detoxification. It is also based on social learning theory and builds on the work of Marlatt and Gordon. The intervention is divided into two components: interpersonal skills training and intrapersonal skills training. The emphasis is, as the title suggests, on educating/training clients in how to revise skills or develop and use new skills in their life. Acquirement of new skills reduces risk of relapse by increasing self-efficacy. Challenging and modification of thoughts about alcohol is also part of the work. The authors suggest that the model can be used in an outpatient setting with minor modifications which include reordering of the sessions according to the challenges that natural environment and risk situations pose.

This model has been adapted and used in the Project Match trial (Kadden *et al.*, 1995). It has also been used by Kathleen Carroll (1998) for treatment of cocaine abuse. Carroll's treatment manual puts emphasis on three stages of coping behaviour: 'recognize, avoid and cope', and involves coping skills training. It includes three types of sessions (introduction to treatment and CBT, significant other and final/termination session), and covers eight topics (similar to the topics covered by Monti *et al.*, 1989).

### *The cognitive model of substance abuse (Beck et al., 1993)*

Beck first developed a treatment manual for substance abuse in 1977 and in 1993 he fully described his model. He acknowledges the work of Marlatt and Gordon, and his model is similar to the relapse prevention model in many ways. However, he incorporates several concepts from cognitive therapy and the pre-existing models of depression and other disorders. Beck emphasizes the important role of beliefs in the development, maintenance and treatment of substance misuse. The central concept of his model is that the use of a substance (initial or relapse) in a certain situation involves an active decision-making process, for which the individual has, or can, regain control. His model is a general model for substance misuse (not just for alcohol), and for individuals at different stages of treatment or substance use status. The examples used in his book are relevant to stimulant use. The 1977 treatment manual was tested with opioid users in the earlier studies by Woody *et al.* (1983) (please see next section on research evidence).

According to the Beck *et al.* model there are three sets of beliefs involved in substance misuse, as with other mental health conditions (such as eating disorders). They are core beliefs (schemata), drug-related beliefs and automatic thoughts.

1. Core beliefs are basic beliefs that the individual holds about him/herself, important others, and the world, as a result of past experience. These beliefs can be shaped by new experiences, but they influence the individual's interpretation of these experiences.
2. Drug-related beliefs are similar to the expectancies beliefs as described by Marlatt and Gordon, and may be anticipatory (the expectation of a positive experience, e.g. 'a fix is just what I need to have a really good time'), or relief-orientated (the expectation of feeling better or coping better, e.g. 'I can't take this anymore, I need a drink or I'm dead'). He also describes another set of beliefs which are substance related: facilitating beliefs, which give the individual permission to exit ambivalence by using ('once more will not harm me', or 'I have already messed up my treatment, so I might as well go for it').
3. Automatic thoughts are concerned with the current situation, and are usually short-term, fleeting thoughts or images, and are described as short versions of basic beliefs described above, for example 'a hit', 'this is bad', 'I can't cope', or mental images of drugs, alcohol or paraphernalia.

In other words Beck emphasizes that drug beliefs and automatic thoughts are shaped and influenced by who the individual is. These beliefs can be crucial for treatment and recovery. He introduces the use of case formulation (used regularly in models of other disorders), as a means to incorporate all of these beliefs in the treatment plan. He also argues that substance misusers share some common personality characteristics/traits (Figure 2.2).

Beck's cognitive model of addiction proposes that individuals are most likely to use a substance when they encounter certain triggers, which may include internal

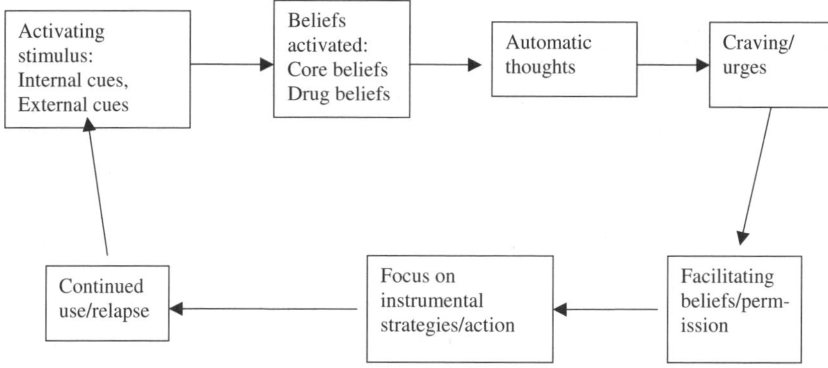


**Figure 2.2** Beck *et al.*'s model (1993).

emotional states (depression, boredom, anger), physical states (withdrawal symptoms, pain) or external circumstances (places or situations associated with drug use). Such triggers activate beliefs, which in turn trigger a process leading to drug use. The first set of beliefs to be activated is the core beliefs, which have an influence on the way that the individual thinks, and his/her attitude to the world. These beliefs in turn activate drug beliefs (positive expectancies from drug use), and both will activate automatic thoughts. Automatic thoughts in turn will activate craving and the urge to use.

Craving is often a strong physical sensation, similar to hunger or thirst. The degree to which people experience craving varies considerably among individuals, circumstances and substance-using status. People who use substances regularly often do not report experiencing craving. However, in the initial stages of abstinence, when they are experiencing withdrawal symptoms, the frequency and strength of craving increases. This is because the individual is trying to resist using, but still thinking about it. Urges are related to the need to exit/terminate cravings. Craving may not be a severe problem for all dependent people, particularly if they are stabilized on substitution treatment. However, they may experience some problems in the early stages of stabilization. The experience of craving and urges may be related to an elaborative sequence of drug-related, as well as automatic thoughts, which is the cognitive element of craving, for example imagining the sequence of buying heroin and using it; thoughts about self-efficacy.

The experience of craving and urges, as well as having thoughts which prohibit using, for example 'I don't need heroin', or 'I don't want to drink', creates dissonance or conflict between different thoughts, or between what the individual needs and wants (e.g. 'a hit right now would make me feel good', or 'I need alcohol to relax'). Dissonance is associated with the experience of anxiety and ambivalence which the individual wants to exit/resolve. Facilitating, or permission-giving beliefs (e.g. 'one more hit won't hurt', or 'I will just have one sip') may follow on from the experience of craving or directly from automatic thoughts, and their role is giving permission to resolve the dissonance.

Once the individual has given himself permission, he focuses on the action of obtaining the substance or substances of choice (instrumental strategies/action). Such a sequence may only result in a 'slip' (lapse), or it may become the trigger for further use and full-blown relapse, if the individual believes that abstinence at this stage is not possible. This continued use provides additional internal and external cues for further activation of beliefs, and so on, reinforcing continued use. For example, the pharmacological effects of drugs are internal cues for use (either to maintain the good mood after using cocaine, or the day after to recover from low mood).

Beck acknowledges that individuals are not always aware of this process, and in particular long-term use (for reasons such as avoidance of unpleasant withdrawal symptoms) can lead to automatized repetitive behaviour (facilitating beliefs, or even action to get drug can follow directly internal or external cues, bypassing the cognitive process). In such cases the primary aim of the therapist is to slow down

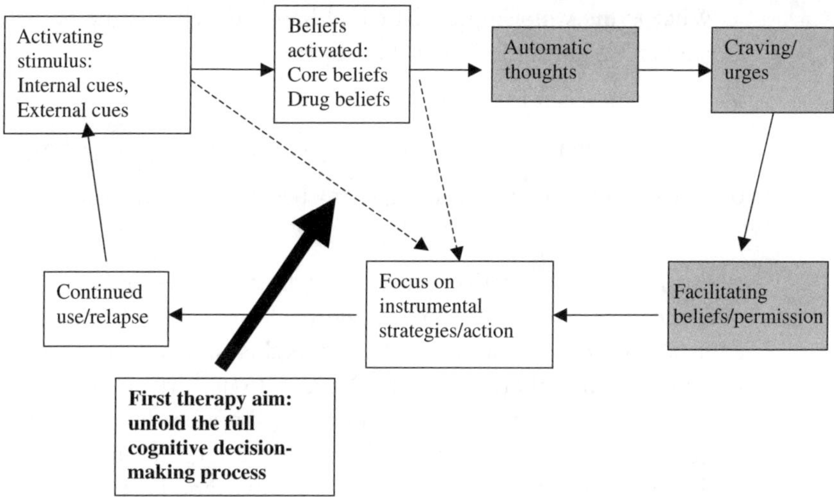


**Figure 2.3** Beck model modified for automatized behaviour.

the short circuit, to enable the individual to become aware of the cognitive process underpinning the decision-making process and to regain control and modify it (Figure 2.3).

Use of the cognitive techniques in cognitive-behaviour therapy is to identify and explore substance-related beliefs. Identifying such beliefs may not be easy for all clients. Substance use is regulated by automatic cognitive processes of which the individuals are mostly unaware, particularly when they are using drugs freely, so they may not be aware of the links between 'beliefs', 'automatic thoughts' and 'craving/urges'. The model presented by Beck, as already mentioned above, requires the therapist to help the client to identify the links in the above chain. This is where cognitive analysis is important. Cognitive analysis involves focusing on the different cognitive elements which include content (what is it about?), processes (rules and heuristics), products (conclusions and attributions following the event), structures (attitudes and expectations), deficiencies and distortions. An accurate assessment of the individual's own perspective of their situation is necessary in order to explore and challenge beliefs, and to generate new and alternative options. This involves breaking the links in the chain at various points, so that new and alternative ways of thinking and acting can be developed to replace the old ones that no longer work. This is achieved by facilitating the client in self-dialogue which involves questioning and challenging one's own beliefs. This will in turn bring an awareness of being able to choose, and to make decisions and changes. Some useful questions to initiate this dialogue are listed below.

***Example***

1. How do I know that what I'm expecting is true?
2. Are there any other ways that I could view this situation?

3. What is the worst thing that could happen? What is the best thing that could happen? What is most likely to happen?
4. What action can I take to deal with the situation?
5. What are the pros and cons of my changing the way I view this situation?
6. What helpful advice would I give my best friend if she were in this situation?

A common characteristic of people who misuse substances is that they often attribute their reasons for using to external factors over which they feel they have no control. The goal of treatment is to explore this conflict by facilitating the individual in understanding their role in the decision to use drugs. This helps individuals to take responsibility for their behaviour and therefore be able to be in control and decide how to move forward. Use of behavioural techniques enables individuals to explore their behaviour and thinking processes, and later on in treatment practice, consolidate new skills acquired.

The Beck model is circular, and it means that substance misuse can predispose to further substance misuse. This does not mean that there are no exit points from this circle. Beck emphasizes the importance of managing lapse or initial use in order not to progress to full relapse or continuous use, in other words to prevent repetition of the cycle. The approach is collaborative with the aim of enabling individuals to learn from their experience, gain control and modify thinking processes, and as a result the related behaviour (Figure 2.4).

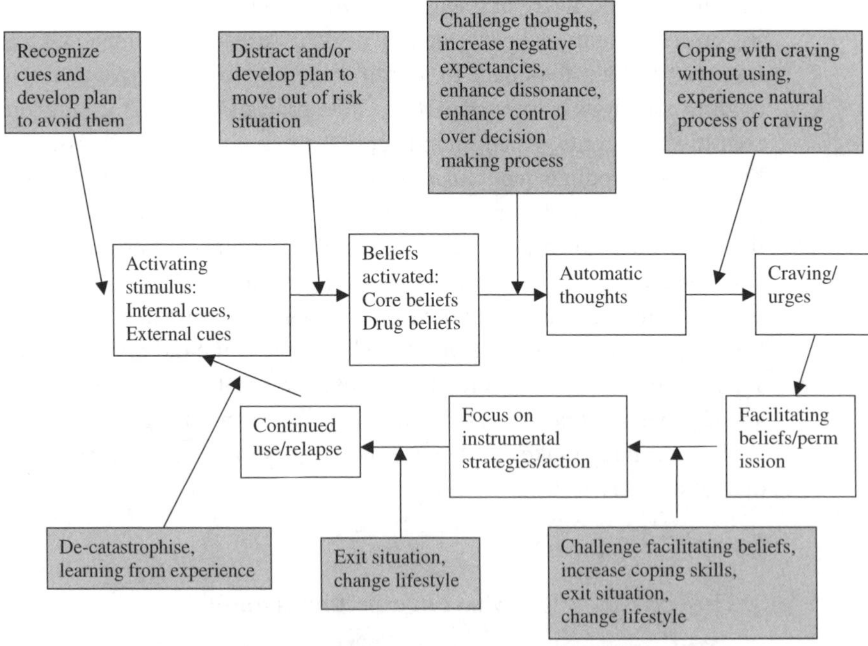


**Figure 2.4** Beck's model with intervention points.

## ▶ Research evidence on cognitive-behavioural therapies in addiction

The psychological treatment of substance misuse is embedded in behavioural and cognitive theories. Its effectiveness is well established, and CBT is now the main treatment approach in alcohol, stimulant and cannabis dependence (Curran and Drummond, 2006). CBT in addiction is based on the principle that addictions are learned behaviours that are capable of being modified. Cognitive approaches primarily aim to change addictive behaviour through changes in faulty cognitions (e.g. dysfunctional beliefs) that serve to maintain the behaviour, or through the promotion of positive cognitions (e.g. self-efficacy) or motivation to change behaviour (Beck *et al.*, 1993). Commonly used approaches are cognitive therapy, relapse prevention and motivational enhancement therapy. Behavioural approaches primarily aim to modify behaviours underpinned by conditioned learning: classical and operant conditioning. Such approaches are many and varied, but include interventions aimed at extinguishing classically conditioned responding (e.g. cue exposure and response prevention), or are based on instrumental conditioning (e.g. community reinforcement or contingency management) in which positive non-drug taking behaviours are positively reinforced. Behavioural approaches involving aversive conditioning are historically important mainly in the alcohol treatment field, and have some evidence of efficacy, but are not used mainly for ethical reasons.

Psychological interventions that incorporate cognitive and behavioural techniques have been shown to be effective in reducing or maintaining abstinence from most forms of substance misuse in a number of studies, either alone or in conjunction with pharmacological interventions. Psychosocial interventions is a term often applied to therapies that aim to assist substance misuse behaviour change such as CBT and motivational interviewing (MI), therapies which are evidence based and have clear underlying principles (Wanigaratne *et al.*, 2005). The evidence on the effectiveness of psychosocial interventions that incorporate cognitive and behavioural techniques in several of the main substances of dependence discussed in this chapter is summarized below.

### *Alcohol*

Psychological interventions based on psychological theories of addictive behaviour are the main treatment approach in alcohol treatment (Curran and Drummond, 2006). A recent review of the effectiveness of treatment for alcohol problems reported that cognitive-behavioural approaches to specialist alcohol treatment offer the best chances of success of treatment effectiveness, and psychosocial interventions can be delivered at a reasonable cost and have wider social cost savings (Raistrick, Heather and Godfrey, 2006). The effectiveness of various treatment modalities were established in this review. Opportunistic brief alcohol interventions, which primarily involved motivational enhancement techniques, are effective in reducing alcohol consumption among hazardous and harmful drinkers to low risk levels. This is now widely seen as an important public health measure to reduce hazardous and harmful alcohol use, and is primarily employed in people identified in routine medical care settings (e.g. primary care, accident and emergency) (Raistrick, Heather and Godfrey, 2006).

The effectiveness of treatments most commonly used in specialist alcohol or addiction services for those with moderate or severe alcohol dependence was also established in this review. These treatments, which come under the broad heading of CBT, included community reinforcement approaches (CRA), social behaviour and network therapy (SBNT), behavioural self-control training (BSCT), coping and social skills training and cognitive-behavioural marital therapy (CBMT), all of which showed evidence of effectiveness as treatment for alcohol problems. Cue exposure (CE) was said to show promise as a treatment method, particularly when combined with a broader CBT programme. The review argued that there is good evidence for the effectiveness of relapse prevention (RP), a CBT treatment first described by Marlatt and Gordon (1985), and that the set of treatment principles and techniques that encompass RP should be incorporated in all specialist alcohol treatments. The authors recommend that more trials are needed of CBT modalities compared to non-CBT treatments (Raistrick, Heather and Godfrey, 2006).

A large systematic review of alcohol treatment outcome research, known as the 'Mesa Grande' (Miller, Wilbourne and Hetema, 2003), included 381 randomized controlled treatment trials. For each treatment modality, scores weighted for methodological quality and outcome were summed across studies to produce a cumulative evidence score (CES), and presented in rank order in a table containing the 48 treatment modalities included in the review. Many of the treatment modalities that had the highest positive scores, hence a large amount of evidence supporting the approach, were psychosocial interventions rooted in cognitive-behavioural theory. These included, in order of rank, brief interventions, motivational enhancement, community reinforcement, self-change manuals, behavioural self-control training, behaviour contracting (also known as contingency management), social skills training, behavioural marital therapy, aversion therapy and cognitive therapy. There is also good evidence that outcomes can be improved when psychosocial treatments (notably relapse prevention, CBT and MET) are combined with acamprosate (Feeney *et al.*, 2002) and naltrexone (O'Malley *et al.*, 1992). However, not all patients respond to these drug treatments (Lingford-Hughes, Welch and Nutt, 2004).

### Stimulants

Psychosocial interventions are the main treatment for dependence on stimulant drugs, including cocaine, crack cocaine and amphetamines (Curran and Drummond, 2006). At present, there is no evidence that any pharmacological treatments can enhance outcome in stimulant treatment (Lingford-Hughes, Welch and Nutt, 2004). Various behavioural treatments have been supported by evidence as effective (Curran and Drummond, 2006), including CBT (Carroll, 1998), relapse prevention (Carroll *et al.*, 1994), motivational interviewing (Stotts *et al.*, 2001), contingency management (Higgins *et al.*, 1993, 1994; Preston *et al.*, 2001) and community reinforcement approaches (Higgins *et al.*, 1993). Contingency management has been shown to be especially effective, particularly when combined with intensive behavioural therapy

(Higgins *et al.*, 2003). For cocaine dependence, a recent systematic review found that community reinforcement approaches plus incentives were effective (Roozen *et al.*, 2004). Both cognitive therapy and contingency management are effective treatments for cocaine-dependent clients in methadone maintenance programmes. However, the combination of these therapies is no more effective than either alone (Rawson *et al.*, 2002). In a recent study of 214 regular amphetamine users who received brief cognitive-behavioural intervention, there was a significant increase in the likelihood of abstinence from amphetamines among those receiving two or more treatment sessions. Reduction in amphetamine use was also accompanied by significant improvements in a number of outcomes including benzodiazepine use, tobacco smoking, polydrug use, injecting risk-taking behaviour (Baker *et al.*, 2005). Relapse prevention has been shown to be effective in promoting abstinence from stimulant drugs over longer periods (Carroll *et al.*, 1994).

### *Benzodiazepines*

There is some evidence to support the effectiveness of CBT in benzodiazepines dependence treatment (Otto *et al.*, 1993; Vorma *et al.*, 2002). However, it is not clear whether psychological treatments are a helpful addition to those who are dependent on benzodiazepines following long-term use of prescribed doses of these drugs, and who are receiving support to gradually reducing their dose over time (Curran and Drummond, 2006). In a study of older adults who had taken benzodiazepines every night for an average of 17 years, 80 % were able to stop taking them following a gradual reduction in dose and information about sleep hygiene (Curran *et al.*, 2003).

Another population uses benzodiazepine, often at very high doses, alongside other drugs. Benzodiazepines may be taken by drug misusers to reduce the come down from crack or to prolong the effects of heroin (Lingford-Hughes, Welch and Nutt, 2004). Very little is known about treating illicit benzodiazepine use by polydrug users (Curran and Drummond, 2006).

### *Opioids*

There is extensive evidence from randomized controlled trials (RCTs) for the effectiveness of pharmacotherapies for opioid dependence, and maintenance agonist treatment, particularly methadone maintenance, is currently the main treatment approach for opioid dependence in most developed countries (Faggiano *et al.*, 2003). As a result of this, psychosocial treatments have been evaluated mainly as an adjunct to methadone maintenance in the majority of studies, rather than as an alternative. A recent systematic review of standalone psychosocial treatments for opiate dependence (Mayet *et al.*, 2004) found that 'enhanced outreach counselling' and contingency management had significantly better outcomes than standard therapies. But these effects were not sustained in the longer term. The authors' conclusion was that in opiate dependence 'at present psychosocial treatments alone are not adequately proved treatment modalities or superior to any other type of treatment'.

A wide range of psychosocial interventions has been applied as adjunctive therapy in pharmacological treatments of opioid dependence. The most commonly applied approaches are currently various forms of cognitive-behavioural therapy. Amato *et al.* (2004a) examined 12 studies comparing eight different psychosocial interventions plus methadone maintenance treatment (MMT), with MMT alone. This review showed additional benefit of psychosocial intervention in terms of reduced heroin use during treatment, but not in terms of retention in MMT or improved outcome at follow-up.

Another recent review of psychosocial interventions in pharmacotherapy of opioid dependence found that CBT in adjunct to MMT can be efficacious, and can produce beneficial clinical and social outcomes (Drummond and Perryman, 2006). However, the authors note that the eight studies reviewed were heterogeneous, they do not always report significant outcomes on a number of important measures, and the studies vary quite markedly in the aims of the intervention and models of CBT applied. The largest number of RCTs ($N = 15$) and the greatest evidence of effectiveness was found in relation to contingency management plus MMT. Most of these studies show positive treatment outcome effects in relation to reduced illicit drug use. There is also evidence of effects on improved attendance at treatment services, treatment compliance, at least for the duration of the CM. The longer term impact of CM is, however, unclear, as is its cost effectiveness. One study (Iguchi *et al.*, 1997) suggested that CM was not effective in a subset of severe drug abusers. Therefore, these clients may benefit from more intensive psychosocial therapy in conjunction with methadone treatment. CM is also a form of behavioural intervention. However, the main difference between CBT and CM is that the former requires more face-to-face client contact, and arguably more therapist skill and training to deliver. So in comparing the relative cost effectiveness of CBT and CM it is possible that the extra cost of therapist training and time for CBT may be offset by the cost of monetary or other incentives in CM. This is an important area for future study.

In comparison to psychosocial intervention research in MMT, relatively little has been carried out in the context of buprenorphine maintenance, perhaps simply as it is a relatively new approach compared to MMT. Of the research that has been conducted, the effect of CM in buprenorphine treatment appears consistent with the effect of CM in MMT. While it is clearly important to study similarities and differences between the effects of psychosocial intervention in MMT and buprenorphine maintenance, it is unclear if the effects of psychosocial treatments differ between these two forms of pharmacological maintenance therapy.

Overall in relation to CBT in the context of agonist maintenance treatments (including MMT and buprenorphine maintenance), CM appears to have greater evidence of effectiveness than standard CBT, at least from studies mainly conducted in the US. However, it is likely that CBT will have a more important role in the treatment of identified psychiatric co-morbidity, including depression, anxiety and post-traumatic stress disorder, all of which are common in MMT populations. This will be most likely to help after people are well engaged in the drug maintenance regime. But it is also likely that motivational enhancement techniques will have a role in encouraging engagement in MMT. More research on motivational techniques specifically in this context is needed.

Naltrexone is an opioid antagonist which aims to reduce relapse by blocking the effects of opioids. Minozzi *et al.* (2006) examined 10 studies of naltrexone for opioid dependence and found that naltrexone maintenance, with or without psychosocial intervention, was more effective than placebo alone in reducing heroin use and incarceration. However, this review did not provide a clear conclusion regarding the additional benefits of psychosocial intervention combined with naltrexone.

Amato *et al.* (2004b) examined the effect of psychosocial interventions in the context of opiate detoxification from both methadone and buprenorphine. The results based on eight studies showed benefits of a variety of psychosocial interventions in terms of completion of treatment, outcome at follow-up and treatment compliance, but not in terms of heroin use during treatment. Drummond and Perryman (2006) found some studies that combined psychosocial interventions with opioid withdrawal treatment in the recent review. Overall, these showed that both CBT and CM improved treatment outcome compared to withdrawal alone, with more studies on CM than on CBT.

### *Polysubstance use*

There is some research examining the effectiveness of psychosocial interventions with polysubstance users. A recent review reported that community reinforcement and contingency management approaches have been shown to be superior to drugs counselling and 12-step approaches, and that a range of family interventions have also been shown to be effective (Wanigaratne *et al.*, 2005). But there is a need for more research on psychological interventions for polydrug misuse, and also for psychiatric co-morbidity, and these populations are often excluded from randomized controlled trials in addiction research.

### *Misuse of medication for pain control*

It is clear that some patients who have been prescribed opiates, including morphine or oxycodone for pain relief, may become dependent. This area has recently been reviewed by the Pain Society (2004). Little is known about the best psychological treatment for this group (Curran and Drummond, 2006).

### *Conclusions*

The evidence suggests that psychosocial interventions that incorporate a range of cognitive and behavioural techniques can be effective in treating a range of substance use disorders. However, there are limitations in the conclusions that can be reached. CBT is a complex approach, treatment effectiveness depends on a number of key factors including the quality of the intervention, the training of the therapists delivering the intervention, therapeutic alliance and adherence, all of which are important determinants of outcome. It is also unclear what the most effective method of delivery of CBT, or the key 'active ingredients', or the optimal 'dose' of intervention is. This type of 'dose' and process research has been more fully carried out in relation to other mental disorders, and this research should be conducted in the addiction field. Therefore, greater clarity on the precise methods of psychosocial intervention is needed in future research. The majority of the research has also taken place in the US and there is a limited evidence base in UK clinical settings, especially for contingency management and community reinforcement approaches, which are rarely used in the UK at present (Wanigaratne *et al.*, 2005). Hence, more research is needed outside of the US on psychosocial interventions so generalizability can be established to other treatment systems and countries. There is also limited evidence on the cost effectiveness of psychological treatment in UK clinical settings. The cross-cultural implementation and testing of psychosocial interventions would be assisted by publication of treatment manuals used in research studies.

## Proposed model of cognitive-behaviour therapy in addiction

Cognitive-behaviour therapy as presented in this book is a short-term, focused psychotherapy, which addresses specific problem areas of substance use. It may be particularly useful for therapists helping individuals to deal with some of the practical and more immediate aspects of their substance use problems, which are crucial to making progress in dealing with more fundamental aspects of their problems. However, it is not a definitive treatment, and it does not explore or resolve some of the deeper and more pervasive problems that some people may experience in association with their substance use.

According to the cognitive perspective, it is the individual's interpretation of the event which is crucially important, and this can affect an individual's feelings, emotions and behavioural responses. Cognitive-behaviour therapy is a collaborative approach in which the therapist and client explore alternative ways of looking at a situation in order to develop alternative options. Cognitive and behavioural techniques are integrated in the practice of the treatment, and are based on the formulation. It is a structured, problem-orientated approach, which makes it more collaborative, although it has an educational component. Out-of-session assignments based on the techniques rehearsed during the session, and graded achievable aims are key to the success of the treatment, because they enhance an individual's self-efficacy (Figure 2.5).

As already said above, this model is not new. It is based on previous models: Carroll's manual for the treatment of cocaine dependence (Carroll, 1998) and Beck's cognitive model (Beck *et al.*, 1993).

**a.** We have used Carroll's format for the topics. However, we have added a number of elective topics. This approach, although descriptive and practical, can be flexible and adapted to the individual needs of the client.

**b.** The cornerstone for understanding the client's needs and cognitive profile is case formulation/conceptualization as presented by Beck. Case formulation brings together past experiences and associated beliefs (schemas), with the current pattern of use, associated drug beliefs and coping skills, in the form of a

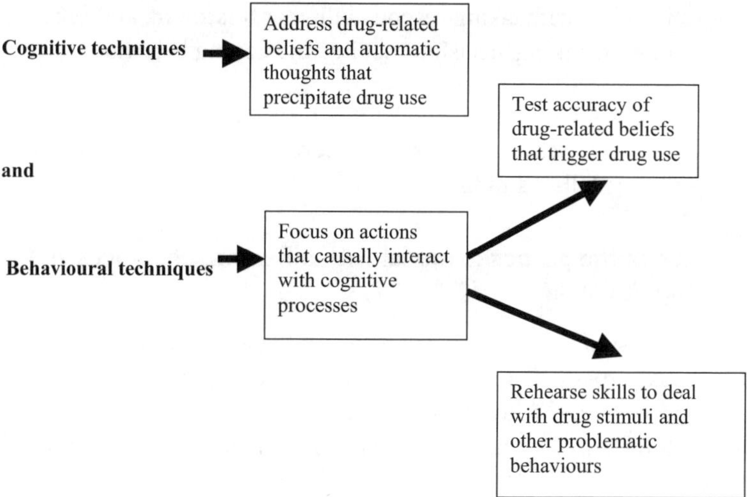


**Figure 2.5** Cognitive and behavioural techniques.

hypothesis that should be shared with the individual and reviewed regularly throughout treatment.

c. Beck's model of substance abuse is central to the treatment model presented here. Our aim is to match core and elective topics to specific exit points from the circle of use (Figure 2.6).

d. We use Carroll's motto, 'recognize, avoid and cope', as a central guide for the treatment strategy.

e. We emphasize that the first and crucial aim for the therapist is to help the individual to understand that use of the substance involves a decision-making process. This is particularly important for individuals whose substance use is largely an automatized behaviour. Acknowledgement of one's own decision-making process

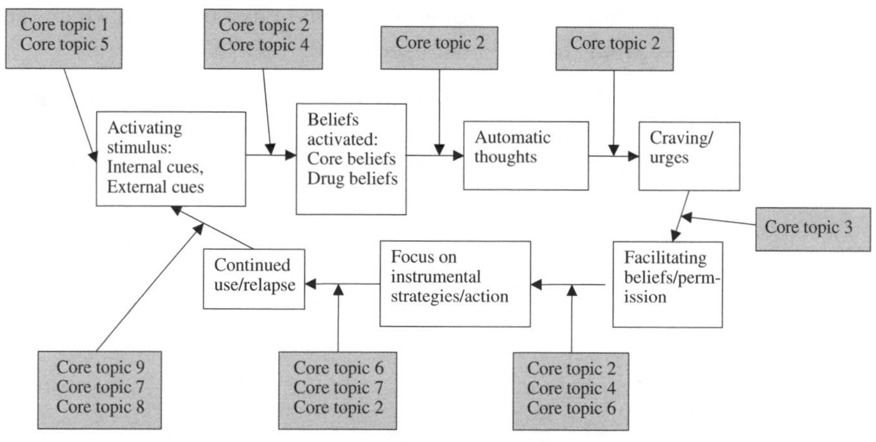


**Figure 2.6** Beck's model with core topics.

is linked with taking responsibility for treatment, and finally gaining control over one's thinking, decision-making and coping behaviour.

This CBT treatment model has three critical components: (i) case formulation based on functional analysis and developmental history; (ii) cognitive restructuring and (iii) skills training.

## Use of the proposed model with different substances and treatment populations

The rest of this chapter will focus on the application of the model described in this book across different substances and client groups, and offer advice on when, how and what to modify, in an explicit way.

Substances of misuse differ from each other mainly in three domains:

1. *Psychopharmacological properties*: pharmacological properties are related to the psychotropic effect of the substance, and therefore influence the user's expectancies from the use of the substance. These expectancies are specific to the substance, and to a degree, are common to all users of the substance, that is all stimulant users expect enhancement of physical energy. However, expectancies are shaped by the user's individual experience of the substance, and will therefore depend on individual needs, that is for some users, stimulants improve social skills, for others this might not be so important.
2. *Legal status*: the legal status of a drug is related to its social acceptance. This has a direct impact on its availability, and therefore the type of risky situations encountered in the cycle of use (see Beck model). Legal status is also associated with lifestyle changes that the client is required to undertake to maintain abstinence. For example, the use of alcohol is culturally accepted and alcohol is widely available in the community. Reminders are widespread and therefore difficult to avoid, even for an individual with a stable family and social background. On the other hand, heroin is illegal, so an individual who has a stable lifestyle might find it easier to avoid exposure to reminders and risky situations which can lead to drug use (i.e. avoid circle of other users).
3. *Treatment aims and philosophy*: treatment aims and philosophy may be different for different substances, that is harm minimization versus abstinence. Treatment options and settings might also be different. Substitution treatment is available for opioid users (i.e. for heroin users) but not for stimulant users (i.e. cocaine users). Outpatient/community service (rightly or wrongly) continues to be the main service provided for opioid users, whereas inpatient detoxification, day services and residential rehabilitation are more commonly available for alcohol-dependent clients. For clients with both problems inpatient treatment might be more easily available.

It is important to emphasize that the above categorizations are generalizations. We have already mentioned that individual experiences, lifestyle and needs are unique for each client, thus the importance of a detailed assessment (see Chapter 5). For any treatment, but in particular for CBT, successful outcome depends on the ability and enthusiasm of the therapist to work with the details that make the application of the CBT model unique for each individual.

### *Alcohol*

As already mentioned above, alcohol use is culturally accepted in Western societies by most communities. This might not be the case in societies where religious beliefs or cultural norms advocate a different view. Issues such as use of alcohol by other family members or in certain official situations (e.g. weddings, religious celebrations, social events) should be taken greatly into consideration when assessing and later in planning treatment sessions and overall treatment strategy.

The treatment aim of most interventions for alcohol-dependent clients is abstinence. Although controlled drinking is an alternative aim, it is recommended for a minority of clients. Most clients presenting with an alcohol problem require psychosocial intervention.

Clients with a dependence problem require pharmacological treatment. Detoxification (either community or inpatient) is usually facilitated with benzodiazepines (or carbamazepine) (Lingford-Hughes, Welch and Nutt, 2004). Medication can be used for relapse prevention either to reduce craving (accamprosate), or as a blocker (naltrexone in the US and disulfiram). Evidence suggests that pharmacological interventions are more efficient when combined with psychosocial interventions.

The use of CBT therefore is appropriate at different stages of treatment, in different forms and in different settings. It can be used in an individual or group format to prepare individuals for inpatient or community detoxification. It can also be used following detoxification for relapse prevention, and in combination with anti-craving medication or even disulfiram. The role of self-help groups such as AA have been widely recognized and the AA network is available in most countries. CBT therapists should be sensitive not to confuse clients involved with both approaches with conflicting principles or theoretical concepts.

The whole model as presented in this book can be used in different settings (e.g. community or residential, while the client is still drinking or following the attainment of abstinence). The order of topics and the number of sessions for each topic may differ depending on the individual, and/or the setting or phase of the treatment programme. As will be seen later, the order of topics will depend on the assessment.

Co-morbidity with depression and anxiety is very common, therefore the relevant elective topics might be very important. Low self-esteem is also a common complicating factor that may need to be addressed.

### *Stimulants*

Psychosocial interventions are the treatment of choice. Community services are the main type of service available, with inpatient detoxification and residential rehabilitation appropriate only for very few (usually those who use other substances too). Community treatments for stimulant misuse/dependence are usually in settings which are distinct and separate from opiate treatment services. Services may offer a mix of tier 2 and tier 3 services: the former focusing on engagement and harm reduction; and the latter on structured care planned treatment. Interventions using CBT are a key component of these services and may be delivered alongside complementary therapies such as acupuncture and aromatherapy. The model presented in this book can be applied as it stands in either individual or group settings. Emphasis on enhancing motivation and engaging clients in the early days of treatment is crucial. Mental health complications of stimulant use are common and include depression, self-harm and psychosis, therefore the relevant elective topics would be very helpful.

The presence of withdrawal symptoms and their effect on the user are not so prominent as with alcohol or heroin users. Therefore stimulant users may believe that they are not dependent. Exploration of issues of control and uncovering the decision-making process may be more compatible with the user's understanding of the problem. Craving may be very strong, so the relevant core topic in combination with recognition of high-risk situations/stimulus may be a high priority in order to enhance confidence and self-control.

### *Benzodiazepines*

The treatment for clients who are dependent only on benzodiazepines has similarities with the approach used for alcohol users, as well as opioid users. Substitution treatment with prescription of a long-acting benzodiazepine (diazepam) to an equivalent dose of all misused benzodiazepines is available. The aim of treatment though is different. Maintenance prescribing is not advisable as there is limited evidence for its efficacy (Models of Care, NTA, 2002; Department of Health Guidelines, 1999). The aim of prescribing should be detoxification, therefore psychological management is crucial to help clients detoxify and maintain abstinence.

The prevalence of co-morbid depression and anxiety with or without sleep problems is high; therefore the relevant elective topics should be considered and included in the treatment plan.

### *Opioids*

In the UK, treatment provided follows the harm minimization philosophy, with major emphasis on early engagement in treatment, retention and reduction of harm to the individual and society. Services are mainly community services, organized around substitution prescribing. Individual drug counselling, otherwise called 'drug keyworking' is closely linked with safe and effective substitution treatment. There is, however, great variability in what this term refers to. The pharmacological interventions used in opiate substitution treatment have a substantial evidence base. Methadone maintenance has been proven effective in reduction in illicit drug use, mortality, criminality, mental health symptoms and HIV risk behaviour (Farrell *et al.*, 1994; Ward, Mattick and Hall, 1997; Marsch, 1998; Lingford-Hughes, Welch and Nutt, 2004). More favourable outcomes from methadone maintenance treatment are associated with doses above 60 mg daily, length of time in treatment, with significant improvements in those engaging for greater than three months (Hubbard *et al.*, 1989), treatment provided by services that are well structured and organized, and treatment delivered with psychosocial interventions. Buprenorphine maintenance has been shown to be broadly comparable with methadone maintenance except at higher doses of methadone where the outcome may be more favourable for methadone. Community detoxification is offered to those with favourable social support and no complicating clinical features. Inpatient treatment offers detoxification, stabilization of drug use and detailed assessment of substance misuse/mental health problems.

CBT can be incorporated into the above treatment settings. The experience of the UKCBTMM trial suggests that it is easier to provide the whole model within services that clients are accustomed to receiving keyworking, with the CBT added in the form of specific appointments. It is also easier to implement the model with clients who are well engaged in treatment, are stable on substitution treatment and who have ready made some changes in their lifestyle. This is not because CBT model cannot be effective in the earlier stages of treatment, but possibly because opioid users attending statutory services are chaotic, and for those who are not experienced or adapted to having some structure in their treatment, implementation of a structured programme may be challenging.

The principles of CBT may be useful from the early stages in treatment. The collaborative philosophy of the approach can empower clients to take responsibility for their treatment and participate in developing a collaborative treatment plan. Sessions on enhancing motivation (see Chapter 6) and use of Socratic questioning as the main interviewing technique can be beneficial for engaging the client in treatment, modifying risky behaviour early in treatment, and to shift towards change later in treatment, where the early successes of maintenance treatment may become obscured by lack of progress. Modified elective topics on treatment compliance can be used early on in treatment too. The full model can then be implemented by identifying and exploring coping with stimulus conditions, and coping with craving and thoughts. Later on, topics on assertiveness, problem solving and lifestyle changes are crucial for maintaining stability in treatment. Other elective topics on how to reduce criminal behaviour, or coping with boredom are also relevant for this group of clients.

The model may be used for those who are still using in addition to their prescriptions, in the same way as it is used with alcohol and stimulant users. For those who are stable on substitution treatment, the model can be used as for those who had achieved abstinence (with more emphasis on relapse prevention).

Within tier 3 prescribing services of Models of Care (NTA, 2002), the model can be:

- Combined with keyworking. The therapist should then focus on reviewing drug use and social problems, including housing and legal problems. Advice on health issues and provision of liaison services with health services, child care and the legal system should be provided as appropriate.

- Be offered by a different member of staff in addition to regular keyworking sessions.
- Be offered by separate services, usually nonstatutory services (depending on the local configuration of the service network). In the same way, the CBT model can be incorporated with Home Office initiatives (Drug Intervention Programmes), either as individual counselling or as a group intervention.

### *Polysubstance use*

Nowadays, the majority of clients attending treatment services are using more than one substance (even excluding cannabis). One of the most important aims of the assessment for such clients is to identify which substance is the one of choice, and how use of different substances is related. The CBT assessment has the same aim. Functional analysis and detailed focus on the pattern of use and related expectations are crucial to understanding how the CBT model may be used. Generalizations such as 'drugs' should be avoided. For each substance, a separate model should be developed (see Chapter 5), although the models will be interacting. Case formulation should include all substances (see Chapter 5).

The therapist should understand and help/educate the client on how use of one substance can be a cue for use of another substance. The challenge usually is that clients dependent on opioids consider heroin to be the only problem because of the associated withdrawal symptoms. Professionals may also adopt this view. They may not consider that cocaine, crack, alcohol, benzodiazepines or weekend use of Ecstasy is a problem (e.g. cocaine use can precipitate heroin use; additional alcohol use with heroin reduces control and precipitates further heroin use, with additional cocaine and benzodiazepine use). Detailed assessment will clarify and unfold the circle of addictive behaviour. The therapist in collaboration with the client will decide what substance will be the treatment starting point (see Chapter 5) (Figure 2.7).

### *Misuse of medication for pain control*

Some clients who attend community drug services requesting treatment for opioid dependence started taking opioids prescribed for pain control (for an acute condition), or started misusing the medication of relatives who were prescribed this type of medication. Others have a history of misusing other substances and at some point were prescribed pain control medication (e.g. following an accident). Such clients have many characteristics in common with other opioid-dependent clients, therefore the same treatment principles may be applied. There is, however, a distinctive group of clients dependent on prescribed opioids for non-cancer pain. Such clients are:

- Socially stable, although family and other relationships may have been affected by the misuse of medication.

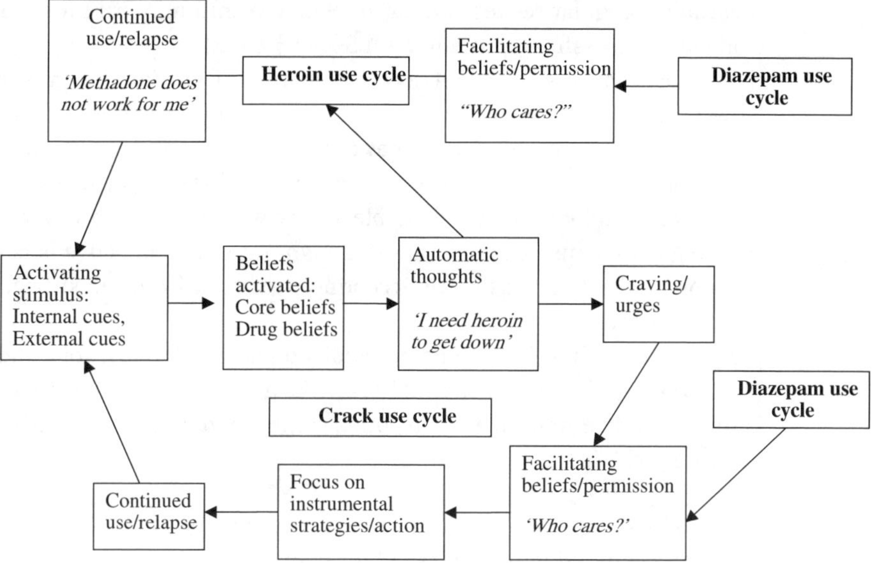


**Figure 2.7** Beck model modified for polysubstance use.

- Misusing prescribed-only medication, and therefore the source for their medication is health services, usually primary care. They come to the attention of the system because they visit their general practitioner requesting higher dosage, or repeat prescriptions too early, or because they approached other professionals for prescriptions. A minority are caught for presenting fraudulent prescriptions.
- Rarely misusing other substances, although they may misuse different types of opioids.
- Not seeking help, because they do not consider misusing medication as problematic or inappropriate. Therefore it is usually the prescribing health professional that seeks advice and support on how to manage and control inappropriately high dosages or repeat prescriptions. Sometimes they are referred to drug and alcohol services following admission or transfer from one treatment service to another, when a new health professional takes over their care and reviews their management.

According to the Models of Care (NTA, 2002), such clients are not the primary focus of tier 3 substance misuse services. Guidelines published by the Pain Society (2004) emphasize that management of such clients should take place within primary care, with the support of the community pain team, and advice by substance misuse services in cases where behaviour indicates addiction. Signs include earlier prescription seeking, claims of lost medication, intoxication, frequent missed appointments and use of other scheduled drugs. Only a small percentage of patients prescribed opioids for pain control will present with the above addictive behaviour. Detailed and multidisciplinary assessment is important for screening those with abuse potentials. Following basic prescribing guidance, which includes long-acting medication, regular revues and liaison with a community pain team, is the cornerstone of a successful treatment (Pain Society, 2004).

Management of such clients can create a lot of tension and misunderstanding between the professionals involved. GPs may find management difficult and complicated, community pain teams may consider that the addictive behaviour aspect of the problem is beyond their expertise, whereas substance misuse services may find that they are under funded and unable to cope with this client group who differ from their regular clients. 'Clients' Lack of insight into their addictive behaviour may be a major barrier to accessing or accepting treatment from the specialist substance misuse services.

Application of the CBT model for addiction is therefore part of a wider treatment plan. Who is going to provide CBT is crucial due to the skills required. First of all it is important to emphasize some points common to all cases of medication misuse and safe prescribing:

- Good liaison between clinicians to ensure reduction of risk for duplicate prescribing and conflicting messages to the client.
- Full reassessment of physical condition that required the prescription in the first place. This assessment should be done sensitively to avoid any judgement and unfair generalizations such as 'there is no problem' or 'he is an addict'.
- Reassessment is crucial to: (i) clarify the severity of the actual physical problem and (ii) identify appropriate medication including alternative treatments available.
- Reassessment should take place at the beginning of treatment, and at regular intervals to reassure the client that the aim of treatment is not only to reduce prescribed medication, but to identify appropriate management.
- Education on the role of medication and concepts such as tolerance and withdrawal symptoms is very important. Paradigms and simple language are very important, but can be challenging to use for a complex problem.
- Measures such as daily pick up of medication or administration by a member of the family may be appropriate.
- Involvement of family members to explain the professional's understanding of the problem, and education in the appropriate treatment plan may be common sense, but can be easily forgotten.

A CBT approach: (a) can help professionals to put the client in the centre of treatment and (b) help the client to take responsibility for his treatment. The collaborative philosophy/approach of CBT can fundamentally contradict traditional medical management. Understanding of the treatment process, graded task assignment and emphasis on a nonjudgemental, but a focused and structured approach, can be challenging for medical colleagues who are not familiar with psychosocial interventions. Magical/unrealistic expectations for the duration of treatment and acceptable interim goals can be problematic. Lack of therapeutic relationship, either in the form of a judgemental and authoritarian approach, or a collusion and defensive approach, can lead to burning out of medical colleagues, and sudden discharge of clients after several years of problematic management, just when all parties start to address the problem.

The CBT addiction model has to incorporate elements of the CBT model for somatic problems. Salkovskis (1995) summarized the common concepts of the CBT conceptualization of most somatic problems:

- Clients believe that their problem has a physical cause or manifestation; this perception may be accurate, exaggerated or completely inaccurate.
- Clients base exaggerated beliefs on observations, which convince them their belief may be true. Exploration of the basis of these beliefs and observations should be part of the assessment, and should be included in the case formulation/conceptualization (see Chapter 4). A separate topic should be added to address such beliefs and modify them. The principles of this topic are similar to the 'coping with cravings' topic of the model (see Chapter 5).
- Clients' somatic problems are threatening in two ways: (a) the degree of handicap or disability arising from the problem and (b) the emotional reaction to the problem, particularly anxiety about its potential causes and consequences, anger and depression.
- The reaction to perceived impairment can include changes in mood, cognitions, behaviour and physiological functioning.
- Problems which originally had a physical cause may later be maintained by psychological factors.

The first step of the CBT approach is a detailed assessment. One of the initial tasks should be exploration of the client's attitude to the referral (Salkovskis, 1995). Emphasis should be on: (a) enhancing motivation; (b) educating the client to increase tolerance (i.e. 'the pain is the same; the tolerance to the medication has increased'); (c) educating the client on the decision-making process; (d) regaining control and (e) developing collaboration. Assessment should also include a detailed enquiry about avoidance behaviour which anticipates symptoms, and any associated thoughts. Avoidance behaviours maintain a client's preoccupation with disease by preventing the client from accessing information, which contradicts negative interpretations of symptoms (Salkovskis, 1995). Use of the techniques of motivational interviewing and Socratic questioning as presented in this model are very appropriate.

## Use of model as an opportunistic intervention in nonspecialist centres

Evidence suggests that there is a high prevalence of substance misuse disorders in the general hospital treatment population as well as in other nonspecialist treatment settings (Kouimtsidis *et al.*, 2003).

Patients admitted to general hospital might suffer from a condition that is not directly related to substance misuse, therefore substance misuse might not be an identified problem on admission. Brief psychosocial interventions have proven to be effective with this population. The main aim of such interventions is to enable patients/clients to seek treatment which mainly focuses on education and enhancement of motivation (Bien, Miller and Tonigan, 1993). The main difficulty with the treatment of such clients is the discrepancy between what the client acknowledges as the problem or obstacle to recovery, and what professional diagnosis and the treatment plan includes. It is a common phenomenon that nonspecialist clinicians would include treatment of alcohol or substance misuse as the most important stage of the treatment, but they may not have the skills to incorporate and implement this stage into the overall treatment plan.

To this effect, the collaborative approach of CBT with the use of Socratic questioning, motivational interviewing, advantages/disadvantages analysis and other techniques as described in this book can be an effective tool for clinicians working in such settings. The proposed model can help them to develop an understanding of the treatment process, and gain the basic skills of how to engage clients and facilitate their treatment pathway. Furthermore, understanding of case formulation and the systematic inclusion of the above techniques into a theoretically based treatment plan can help the clinicians not only to formulate a treatment plan, but also take the very first and crucial steps of engaging a client in a life-changing treatment journey.

## Group therapy

The model in this book can be used in a group format. Certain issues about the group format itself should be decided: Is the group closed or open? How many clients will be involved? Will it be substance specific or across substances? At what stage of treatment will be added for example abstinence or still using? The above issues can dictate the necessary modifications of the model.

The duration of the group sessions should be longer than individual sessions (1 hour or longer). In groups the order of topics is usually prearranged, therefore there is less space for flexibility. Pre-group assessment of participating clients is good practice. The aim is to inform the client about the purpose of the group, basic rules, and more importantly, if possible to develop an individual formulation. Although the above changes, the principles of agenda setting and structure of the session (see Chapter 4) should be followed.

CHAPTER THREE

# Cognitive and behavioural techniques

## Introduction

In this section the main cognitive and behavioural techniques used in therapy will be described in detail. Each technique will be described under the following headings:

- Description of technique
- Example
- What it is useful for – topics/problems for which the technique might be used
- Problems – types of problems/things that go wrong and techniques/solutions.

The techniques can be adapted for the core and elective topics, but certain techniques may be particularly useful for some topics, which will be listed. Some techniques may work better with some clients than others, thus increasing flexibility and adaptability of the treatment to accommodate different clients. The techniques have been divided into cognitive and behavioural groups depending on the focus of the procedure; however, this does not reflect the order in which they should be used. Both cognitive and behavioural techniques are used from the outset.

The order in which the techniques are presented within each group in the book should be used as a guideline for the therapy, some may be used throughout the therapy, whereas others may be more appropriate for the earlier or later stages of therapy, or superficial or deeper analysis. For example, early stage/superficial cognitive techniques include addressing ambivalence and enhancing motivation, and daily thought records; and behavioural techniques include relaxation training and physical exercise. Later stage/deeper cognitive techniques include downward arrow exercise and imagery, and behavioural techniques such as behavioural experiments. Whilst each technique is described separately, it is important to recognize that there will be some overlap and more than one technique may be used to address a problem. Combinations of techniques may be used as merits the circumstances.

It is important to understand that cognitive-behaviour therapy is not just a list of techniques which can be applied in a 'cook book' manner from a menu. Cognitive-behaviour therapy is a strategic approach based upon a background of cognitive and behavioural science which allows the therapist to understand the client's clinical problems and organize the information into a logical and clinically useful formulation. The formulation represents the therapist's understanding of the clinical issues and facilitates the selection of a procedure for intervention. Developing a case formulation involves generating a series of clinical hypotheses, which are tested out through the application of various treatment or intervention methods. It is also important to develop the formulation in collaboration with the client so as to help the client understand the cognitive-behavioural model.

### *Out-of-session assignments*

Treatment takes place within treatment sessions but also during the client's everyday life, initially through home-based exercises, but eventually through lifestyle changes which involve changes in the client's behaviour and thinking styles. The therapist should keep this is mind and plan for sustainable change which may involve being aware of the environment in which the client lives and functions, and how this will help or hinder lifestyle change. Generalization of skills learnt in therapy to everyday life must be thought about and discussed with the client as a problem-solving exercise. Factors that will facilitate and prevent change should be identified by the client and potential solutions generated and implemented. Out-of-session assignments should be set so as to aid generalization and to sustain any progress made within the treatment sessions. This exercise is often poorly carried out, so it should be discussed with clients at an early stage so that they are aware of it, and to promote an honest appraisal of any specific problems that they may encounter. Exercises should initially be simple, easy to perform, clearly described and easily monitored, so that both client and therapist can be clear about whether they have been carried out and what impact they have had. Initially the behaviour of the client needs to be shaped, which means any approximation to completing the exercise should be reinforced with praise and clear feedback given as to how this can be improved. Out-of-session assignments are an extension of the treatment into the client's everyday life, and although they may progress slowly, they are essential for the success of the treatment. Thus, what assignment is given and when and how it will be carried out needs careful thought and discussion. Giving too much that is too complex and vague should be avoided, especially at an early stage in treatment when it may be unlikely to be implemented, and could overload and demoralize the client.

### *List of techniques*

Cognitive techniques:

- Addressing ambivalence and enhancing motivation
- Socratic method
- Daily thought record
- Distraction

- Advantages/disadvantages analysis
- Flashcards
- Downward arrow exercise
- Imagery.

Behavioural techniques:

- Activity-monitoring schedule
- Relaxation training and physical exercise
- Behavioural rehearsal (role-play and reverse role-play)
- Behavioural experiments
- Contingency management.



## Cognitive techniques

### *Addressing ambivalence and enhancing motivation*

An exploration of the client's ambivalence and motivation should be incorporated into the assessment, and addressed as necessary throughout the treatment. Motivational interventions are partly based on Prochaska and DiClemente's process of change model (Prochaska and DiClemente, 1992) and were described by Miller and Rollnick (1992) as 'motivational interviewing'. Essentially this approach aims to work with the client's perception of substance use rather than imposing the therapist's external view of reality. Clients who are rarely in a state where they do not view some aspect of their substance use to be problematic or in need of change, are given encouragement to reflect on the role of the drug in their life. However, if the therapist confronts the individual's view, denial will manifest itself as a defence mechanism. In motivational interviewing, the aim is to lead clients to the point where they propose goals to change their substance use, through a process of helping individuals to explore the positive and negative aspects of their substance use, and developing discrepancy. This latter approach aims to help clients to recognize the discrepancy between their view of themself and their behaviour (e.g. an alcoholic regards himself as being 'a social drinker' but has been arrested for assaulting his partner whilst intoxicated with alcohol). Miller and Rollnick (1992) describe the essential principles and practice of motivational interviewing:

- Express empathy
- Help the client to recognize discrepancies between his/her goals and current behaviour problem
- Roll with the client's resistance rather than oppose it directly
- Explore consequences of action and inaction
- Communicate free choice

- Support self-efficacy by emphasizing personal responsibility and the hope of change.

The intervention depends on the individual's stage of change. According to Prochaska and DiClemente (1992), there are five stages of change:

- *Pre-contemplative stage*: the individual is unaware of the problems associated with drug or alcohol use and is often surprised rather than defensive that the topic is being raised. The aim at this stage is to increase awareness of the potential problems.
- *Contemplative stage*: the individual is developing an awareness of the problem but is ambivalent about change. The aim is to help the client to make a decision that on balance change is needed.
- *Determination stage*: the therapist is mainly helping the client to enter the most appropriate form of recovery help by providing a menu of options for change (e.g. choice of treatment agency) and making practical preparations for change (e.g. arranging time off work, child care).
- *Action stage*: a whole range of options of intervention can be used but usually at this stage the client is actively engaged in the change process and little input is required in motivational terms except to reinforce the client's positive decision and determination.
- *Maintenance stage*: the main focus of therapy is identifying methods of consolidating gains and preventing relapse. Often this involves identifying longer term lifestyle modification towards maintaining change. If relapse occurs, the therapy is directed at helping the client to re-engage in the treatment process.

For more detailed presentation of strategies to enhance and maintain motivation please see Chapter 6, Section 'Core topic 1'.

***Summary of motivational interviewing*** Work with the client's ambivalence and perceptions of his/her substance use. Guide the client to the point where he/she proposes goals to change substance use.Five stages of change: pre-contemplative, contemplative, determination, action and maintenance.

Principles of motivational interviewing

- Express empathy
- Help client recognize discrepancies between goals and behaviour
- Roll with client's resistance
- Explore consequences of action and inaction
- Communicate free choice
- Support self-efficacy.

### *Socratic method*

The Socratic method is a guided form of self-discovery and awareness facilitated by the therapist. It is based upon the method of Socrates the Ancient Greek philosopher who sought to illuminate the truth by question and answer, responding to each question with a question until the respondent came to the answer to their own enquiry. It establishes a nonjudgemental atmosphere and thus facilitates collaboration between client and therapist. Thinking is shaped through active questioning and selective reflection. It allows clients to develop an awareness of their own beliefs and behaviours. By asking such questions clients develop an insight into their thought processes and how these influence their emotions and behaviour. Accordingly the client becomes aware of inappropriate beliefs and is helped to challenge them and change the behaviour. The guided questioning should be balanced by clarification, feedback and education based on the theme of the discussion. Questions should be phrased in such a way as to stimulate thought and increase awareness, rather than requiring a correct answer. Questions can be asked that identify the connection between thoughts and feelings especially when negative automatic thoughts are involved. For example, the client may think that he 'will never be normal' and he is asked to examine how he feels when he has this thought. The therapist can then explore with the client the validity and utility of this thought but this is not achieved by directly challenging the thought. The principles of collaborative empiricism are adhered to by asking questions that support or refute the thought, asking about possible alternative explanations, questioning about the range of consequences of the thought and their impact upon the person and what would be the effects of believing the thought or of changing their thinking.

For more details of this and other cognitive methods see Beck (1995).

### *Example*

| | |
|---|---|
| *Client:* | I can't stop using drugs. It is the only thing that I can do. |
| *Therapist:* | What makes you say this? |
| *C:* | It seems that I cannot think straight when there are drugs around. |
| *T:* | Does this mean that you can think straight when you are in safe situation? |
| *C:* | I don't know. |
| *T:* | What would be a safe situation for you? |
| *C:* | Visiting my friend B who is not using. |
| *T:* | What is different about this situation? |
| *C:* | He is there. I can talk to him if I start craving. |
| *T:* | So talking about craving helps you to cope with it. |
| *C:* | Yes it seems so. |
| *T:* | So you might find it helpful to discuss it with non-using friends. |
| *C:* | Maybe you're right. |

Then move on to a related topic, for example the belief that she is not able to do anything else.

***What is it useful for – topics/problems for which the technique might be used*** This technique should be used throughout the therapy but particularly the following:

- Assessment – formulation
- Challenging beliefs and cognitive distortions
- Identifying and exploring ambivalence and enhancing motivation
- Identifying stimulus conditions, craving and seemingly irrelevant decisions.

***Problems – types of problems/things that go wrong and techniques/solutions*** Too many open-ended questions may lead to a lack of response and no conclusion or formulation of the problem. Being too vague will result in a lack of focus and an inability to formulate a conclusion. For example after questioning the client it might be useful to go back over the main points of the discussion (reflection) and clarify the accuracy of them with the client. Giving feedback on important points, educating the client through presenting the cognitive formulation of the problem and asking the client for views on the formulation.

It is easy for the therapist to slide into being didactic rather than Socratic by giving the answers or direct advice rather than leading clients to come to their own conclusions. For example, the therapist can be tempted to directly challenge a negative automatic thought rather than leading the client to question it.

***Example***

*Client:* It makes me feel sad when I think I'll never get better.
*Therapist:* Of course you'll get better, all the evidence tells us so.

A more productive approach would be for the therapist to respond as follows:

*T:* How would you feel if you thought you would get better?
*C:* I'd feel happier.
*T:* What is it that makes you think you'll never get better, why do you think that?

Then go on to examine the evidence and follow this up with linking the thought about not getting better with the sad emotion, and how the emotion will change depending on the type and nature of the thoughts the client has.

***Summary of Socratic method***

- Guided self-discovery and awareness.
- Facilitated by the therapist.
- Active questioning and selective reflection.
- Aim to develop awareness of beliefs and behaviours.
- Balance with clarification, feedback and education.

### *Daily thought record*

The daily thought record is designed to help clients to examine their own drug-related, or other, beliefs/thoughts in a systematic and objective fashion. It also helps the therapist to understand the client's thought processes. This is usually done using a table split into columns (usually six) which include situation, automatic thoughts/beliefs, emotions, response, outcome and rational response. The aim is for the client to identify and record the situations (external, e.g. activity, place, event, time) or an emotional state which precipitates possible drug use. This enables the client and therapist to examine the sequence leading to drug use, and therefore thought and behaviour patterns which can be modified. The aim of this exercise is firstly to help the client and therapist to identify internal (emotions) and external (situations) drug stimuli, related beliefs and thoughts and behavioural patterns associated with them. Secondly, the exercise provides the information needed to educate clients in the cognitive model and enable them to realize that drug taking is a decision-making process in which they have a choice. Thirdly, and perhaps most importantly it allows clients to become aware of their thought processes and to link them to emotions and behaviour. The process has the added advantage of providing some 'distance' from the thoughts so that the emotional reaction can be slowed and potentially controlled. Thus, clients can become aware of their thoughts and emotions and how they are connected rather than being 'caught up' in the content of their thoughts.

The diary also provides useful scenarios for skills training using the individual's own examples. Through self-learning and self-monitoring clients are enabled to monitor and review their progress, enhance motivation and self-efficacy.

***Example***
See Figure 3.1.

#### *What is it useful for – topics/problems for which the technique might be used*

- Assessment – formulation
- Identifying and dealing with stimulus conditions

| **Situation:** Describe event or distressing physical sensations | **Automatic thoughts/ Beliefs** | **Emotions:** Specify sad, anxious, angry & rate degree of emotion | **Response:** Action taken to resolve situation | **Outcome:** Record changes in thoughts and feelings after action | **Rational response** |
|---|---|---|---|---|---|
| *Sitting indoors at 6pm watching TV, nothing to do, bored* | *I need something to relax me No heroin indoors Nothing changes* | *Anxious 70% Frustrated 60%* | *Had a lager, phoned my friend and went to his place to score* | *Feeling more relaxed Guilty and angry for using* | *Distract, e.g. go for a walk Challenge thoughts, refer to flashcards* |

**Figure 3.1** Example of daily thought record.

- Seemingly irrelevant decisions
- Adapting lifestyle (changes)
- Managing boredom.

***Problems – types of problems/things that go wrong and techniques/solutions***

Diary keeping is unlikely to be an easy task to accomplish initially, and it is important for the therapist to be aware of this and to encourage the client to produce any kind of diary material to get started, so beginning with some common example might be useful, for example road rage. The therapist should attempt to shape the client's behaviour so that any attempts are rewarded and reinforced. Working through an example during the session is helpful as it provides a model for the client to follow. The diary is a useful insight into the client's cognitions, so regular review is necessary to improve diary-keeping skills (e.g. being specific to events, separating thoughts and emotions, recording events as soon as possible after they occur). It is important to help the client to identify the unique characteristics of each situation. A good example to give to the client is that the process of diary keeping can be seen as 'zooming in' on the action and slowing down the motion to study the details, as in a replay of action in a film. Some clients will never be good at keeping diaries, so it may be necessary to employ alternative strategies (in-session techniques, e.g. role-play, advantages/disadvantages analysis, downward arrow exercise and imagery).

### *Distraction*

Distraction may used to help clients to refocus their attention from either internal (emotional states, automatic thoughts, craving) or external drug-related stimuli. Distraction can be either cognitive (changing the focus of attention) or behavioural (engaging in physical activity, housework, gardening). Cognitive distraction involves training clients to focus their attention away from drug-related thoughts and craving by focusing on other thoughts, for example describing surroundings. This is an important skill as it involves the regulation and control of attention. The client should have a number of distraction techniques that can be used in different situations, which should be specific to the client. Systematic training in attention control and attention switching can be achieved through asking the client to attend to various aspects of, or objects within, the environment, and by focusing attention on the same for a set period of time. For example, attending to objects or pictures in a room and then to noises outside, such as traffic. This helps clients to regulate their attentional processes and bring them under control. Subsequently, the client can be asked to focus on internal stimuli by being asked to generate a pleasant visual image or a place or situation. These can be relaxing or pleasant images, such as a tropical beach, or the client's own memories of a positive event, such as an enjoyable meal in a cafe, or restaurant. The client is then asked to describe the situation in great detail whilst building up a vivid mental image. This is carried out a number of times until the client is able to create the mental image vividly and easily. The client should also be asked to imagine other sensory inputs such as how it felt to be in the sunshine on the beach, the noise of the waves and the feel of the sand and so on. In this way all the senses are engaged and can be strongly associated with positive affect by asking the client to endorse positive statements about the situation and elicit positive affective responses to the distracting stimulus. Clients are then taught to switch their attention away from a range of other stimuli to the target-distracting scenario until they are highly competent in being able to do this. Once they are able to do this they can use this internal distraction and attention-switching technique in response to undesirable thoughts and feelings. Thoughts about increased control should also be elicited to reinforce these actions, build the client's feelings of self-efficacy and decrease the expectation of the strength of drug-related experience and thoughts. Distraction can also be achieved through engaging in activities which allow attention to be refocused on these tasks. Such concrete behavioural tasks can be easier for the client to initiate and more easily used as an active coping strategy in the earlier stages of treatment than purely cognitive tasks. Having specific activities for the client to engage in as a form of distraction is useful because they require active concentration, and thus reduce the attentional capacity available for drug-related thoughts. Activities (behavioural) and other interests the client has will also be beneficial in helping to change lifestyle. It is important that clients have a repertoire of both cognitive and behavioural strategies because they may find themselves in situations where it is not possible to engage in some activity, for example recurring situations where the client feels bored and starts thinking about drugs which precipitate craving. The client should also be aware that successful use of distraction can be used to challenge negative cognitions or expectation such as 'I have no control over my behaviour' or 'I'll never improve'.

***Example***
A client's friend comes to visit him at home, takes out heroin and starts to prepare it, but the client cannot leave the flat. One of the coping strategies for this situation could be a distraction plan.

- Go upstairs and listen to favourite songs – distraction plan devised by client to have list of favourite songs
- Stay for 10 minutes or until craving or temptation dissipates
- Go back and check to see if friend is still there, if he is ask him to leave.

***What is it useful for – topics/problems for which the technique might be used***

- Identifying and dealing with stimulus conditions
- Seemingly irrelevant decisions
- Managing boredom.

***Problems – types of problems/things that go wrong and techniques/solutions*** If distraction is going to achieve its goal (i.e. prevent the client from using drugs when craving), it must be effective in distracting the client from craving. Clients may find it difficult to generate ideas initially because of having a lifestyle so focused around drugs. It may therefore be necessary to explore with the client things enjoyed in the past as well as looking for new material. Switching attention may initially be a rather weak strategy in response to physical cravings and will need to be systematically practised and implemented. Combining behavioural and cognitive techniques can be helpful. Sustaining distraction can be difficult and may be abandoned or perceived as a 'stop gap' approach, whereas the client needs to view the use of this method as leading to a regaining of control over thoughts and feelings, which may be a long process.

#### *Summary of distraction*

- Used to help client to refocus attention from either internal or external drug related stimuli.
- Can be cognitive or behavioural or combination.
- Should be detailed and if possible rehearsed in safe environment for maximum effectiveness.
- Client should have repertoire of cognitive and behavioural distraction techniques that can be used in different situations which should be specific to the client.

### *Advantages/disadvantages analysis*

This involves making a list of the advantages and disadvantages of using drugs, and re-evaluating drug use overall. This is done using a four-cell matrix with the advantages and disadvantages of using and not using drugs (see example). This exercise can be used within the session, or as an out-of-session assignment. It is important that the client records his/her own view of advantages and disadvantages, and not that of the therapist or society more generally, so cognitive analysis (i.e. examining beliefs and cognitive distortions using the Socratic method) will facilitate obtaining an accurate representation of the client's views. This task is helpful for facilitating clients to generate alternative views and challenge assumptions they may have, by examining the issue from a number of different perspectives. When the analysis is successful, the client should have a more accurate, objective and balanced view of substance use than was previously held. Statements generated by this technique can be used as material for other techniques such as 'flashcards' or 'downward arrow exercise' and may be particularly helpful in goal setting and enhancing motivation as part of each session.

#### *Example*

See Figure 3.2.

#### *What is it useful for – topics/problems for which the technique might be used*

- Identifying and exploring ambivalence and enhancing motivation
- Problem solving
- Adapting lifestyle (changes).

|  | Stop using heroin | Continue using heroin |
|---|---|---|
| **Advantages** | *More money*<br>*Be clean*<br>*Have a normal life*<br>*Better relationship with family* | *Meeting friends*<br>*Having a good time*<br>*Not feeling pain*<br>*Getting money* |
| **Disadvantages** | *Losing friends*<br>*Losing money*<br>*Having withdrawals*<br>*Boredom* | *Spending too much money*<br>*Make partner angry*<br>*Being dependent* |

**Figure 3.2** Example of advantage/disadvantages analysis.

### *Problems – types of problems/things that go wrong and techniques/solutions*

Typically, clients maintain beliefs that minimize the disadvantages and maximize the advantages of using drugs. At the same time the client will be aware of socially acceptable answers and may be inclined to give these responses in order to satisfy the therapist. Often the client is not deliberately lying or attempting to deceive the therapist, but rather is unaware of their own core beliefs. It is therefore important for the therapist to explore the client's true beliefs, so that an accurate formulation can be made and appropriate modifications made. This analysis may generate contradictory statements, which need to be explored, clarified and feedback supplied. The client may hold several dissonant beliefs. Reassure the client that this is a normal phenomenon which will be explored in treatment. On the other hand, an inaccurate picture of the client's belief system can devalue the treatment because the client's true beliefs are not being addressed, and therefore cognitive modification is not achieved. A downward arrow exercise (see relevant section) may be useful in this analysis. This type of exercise can be useful for exploring ambivalence and for creating dissonance relating to drug use. The reduction of dissonance can help motivate the client to decide to reduce or give up drug use. It can also be helpful to try and engage the client's affective response to the various advantages and disadvantages, so that they come to elicit a positive affect with advantages of not using drugs, and a negative affect with drug use. This goes some way to prevent 'mere intellectualizing' about advantages and disadvantages.

### *Summary of advantages/disadvantages analysis*

- List advantages and disadvantages of using drugs using four-cell matrix.
- Ensure that clients record their own perspective on advantages and disadvantages.
- Important to explore client's true beliefs for accurate formulation and modification.
- May generate contradictory statements which should be explored, clarified and feedback supplied.
- Client may hold several inconsistent beliefs.

### *Flashcards*

Flashcards help clients to use what they have learned in therapy in real-life situations. In a stimulus condition, when clients are faced with their automatic thoughts and drug-related beliefs, they need to remind themselves of how to challenge these thoughts and/or cope. These may be appropriate responses to situations, coping statements or reinforcement of positive consequences of being drug free. Flashcards (3″ × 5″ index cards) should be small, suitable for carrying around, and have the client's own relevant statements listed on them. Flashcards can be used in a range of situations, and for various functions such as aids to memory, challenge inappropriate cognitions and to facilitate and direct goal-directed behaviour and positive action. In effect, they act as an external cue to generate an appropriate internal dialogue and to prompt appropriate beliefs and cognitions. Appropriate self-talk can be very helpful in the self-direction of behaviour in an environment in which the cues are most probably related to inappropriate beliefs or drug use. It should be remembered that they should be focused and functional.

***Example***
When I meet a friend or find myself in the company of friends who use drugs:

- Respond 'no' firmly if offered any drugs
- Don't allow myself to get into any discussion about it
- Leave if the situation becomes difficult.

When I feel that I want to use heroin, think about the advantages of not using:

- More money
- Not in trouble
- Better relationship with wife
- Able to see children again.

***What is it useful for – topics/problems for which the technique might be used***

- Identifying and dealing with stimulus conditions
- Refusal skills/assertiveness
- All-purpose coping plan
- Seemingly irrelevant decisions
- Problem solving
- Adapting lifestyle (changes).

***Problems – types of problems/things that go wrong and techniques/solutions***
It is important to emphasize to clients to remember to carry the cards with

them so that they will have them available when they need them. Some effort may need to be put into creating the cards (clients should make their own cards) and deciding on the most appropriate places to keep them. It is also important to keep this technique for the most important issues, and that the function of each card is understood. Try not to bombard the client with so many cards that they are forgotten or become confusing. An alternative to flashcards may be small posters with the same material displayed in appropriate places in the home.

#### *Summary of flashcards*

- Help clients to use what they have learned in therapy in real-life situations.
- Include appropriate responses to situations, coping statements, rational responses to core/drug-related beliefs.
- Flashcards should be small and have the client's own relevant statements listed on them.
- Keep this technique for most important issues.
- Ensure function of each card is understood.
- Try not to bombard the client with too many cards.

### *Downward arrow exercise*

Clients are often unaware of their own underlying core beliefs, or they may find it difficult to articulate the personal meaning (i.e. what does that mean to you?) of the more accessible and/or acceptable beliefs and thoughts that they experience. It is highly probable that underlying beliefs are reflected in ongoing cognition of which the client may be aware or learn to become aware. By using a Socratic questioning approach, clients are able to access these underlying core beliefs by means of asking questions about their thoughts. Using this method, clients can become aware of underlying fears or concerns, or of what they assume must or should occur. Such beliefs frequently drive their behaviour in absence of their awareness. The downward arrow exercise is a useful means of accessing difficult to reach core beliefs by asking successive variations of the question, 'What does that mean to you?' or 'If that was true what would it mean?'. Examples of this include: de-catastrophizing (e.g. 'What is the worst thing that can happen?'); correcting 'all or nothing' thinking (e.g. 'I'm completely out of control'), overgeneralization (e.g. 'I can't do anything right') and selective attention (e.g. focus of attention on withdrawal-type symptoms). This exercise should be rehearsed and practised during the therapy session with the guidance of the therapist only, so it should not be used outside of the session. Information obtained from the exercise may be used for other techniques or on flashcards to act as a reminder for the client outside of the therapy session. This technique will also frequently reveal the illogical or contradictory nature of the client's beliefs, or failure to consider other options or explanations of events. This lack of cognitive flexibility

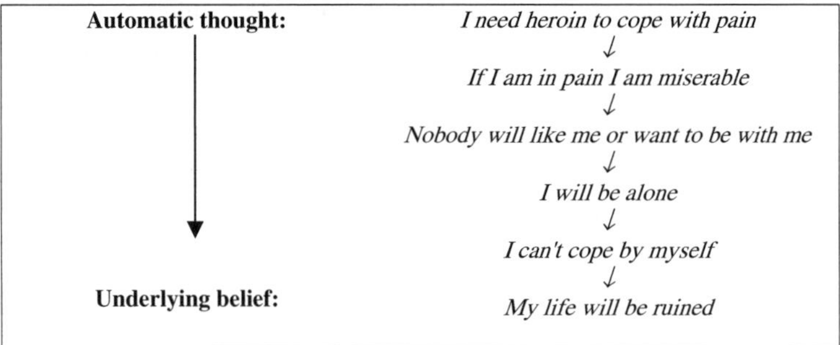


**Figure 3.3** Example of downward arrow exercise.

can be usefully targeted as a therapeutic goal in that the client can investigate other options or interpretations at each stage.

***Example***

See Figure 3.3.

***What is it useful for – topics/problems for which the technique might be used***

- Assessment – identifying beliefs (drug and non-drug-related beliefs)
- Identifying and dealing with stimulus conditions
- Refusal skills/assertiveness
- Seemingly irrelevant decisions
- Problem solving.

***Problems – types of problems/things that go wrong and techniques/solutions***

Problems encountered in using this technique may be once again not getting an accurate picture of the client's real perceptions. The client may get stuck in the process or jump to inaccurate conclusions. If this happens, it can in itself be useful for helping clients to understand their thought processes and their consequences. The therapist may need to address problems encountered in this exercise by using Socratic techniques, that is clarification, feeding back and educating the client using simple examples. Asking clients to go through an example in detail, and to reflect on why they thought in a particular way, what the consequences were, how they could have thought differently and what the result would have been, can be very helpful for facilitating clients to understand the cognitive model.

***Summary of downward arrow technique***

- Useful means of accessing difficult to reach core beliefs by de-catastrophizing, correcting 'all or nothing' thinking, overgeneralization and selective attention.
- This exercise should be rehearsed and practised during the therapy session only.

- Information obtained can be used for other techniques, or on flashcards, to act as a reminder for the client outside of therapy session.

### *Imagery*

Imagery as a technique involves getting the client to imagine specific problematic, drug-or alcohol-related experiences. Imagery can be used retrospectively to 'relive' a past experience (usually the most recent) so as to identify the emotions, thoughts and context associated with the problematic event or experience. For example, going over a relapse situation and identifying the context as to why drinking was resumed. Imagery can also be used prospectively to 'project ahead' to a difficult situation in order to plan an effective coping strategy. It can also be used to overlearn such coping strategies so that they can be implemented more easily.

Imagery is a useful technique for helping clients to explore during therapy, situations encountered in their daily lives and possible outcomes. This is done by encouraging them to relive the experience as though it is happening in the here and now. Mental images in themselves are powerful reminders but can be further enhanced by asking clients to relive the experience using all their senses. Asking how something felt or smelt or tasted or any associated sounds will help reliving across all the senses, although visual imagery is likely to be the strongest. In this way cognitive processes and the affective or emotional reactions involved can be broken down into drug- or alcohol-related beliefs, automatic thoughts, behavioural processes leading to action, and associated feelings. Imagery may be used as an alternative or as well as the daily thought record. It may also be useful for clients who are not good at keeping diaries. Imagery can, in addition, be a powerful technique for challenging thoughts and beliefs, and imagining alternative coping strategies. Imagery is also very useful for rehearsing particular coping strategies, for identifying the positive consequences of their outcome and any potential impediments. It can be used as well to help the client to look at the positive side of a drug-free lifestyle, for example imagining enjoyable activities as alternatives to drug use, and imagining their lives without drugs and anticipating any positive feelings such a lifestyle would have. For clients who have little in the way of a positive drug-free past experience to draw upon, emphasizing the positive element of being drug free is important. Positive imagery can also be a useful way to build client's self-esteem and confidence, by asking them to imagine and experience a positive image or set of behaviours, and eliciting positive comments from the client about themselves. This can be further enhanced by asking the client to try and recreate the positive affect associated with the experience. Cued images can then be used in the future to trigger positive affect and feelings about oneself, while also cueing in positive behaviour.

It cannot be emphasized enough that imagery can be extremely powerful, and should therefore only be used when the therapist and the client feel safe and comfortable enough to practise it. Mental images are often a powerful cue to emotions, often more so than words or descriptions and there is the possible risk of triggering powerful emotions unexpectedly. This means giving the client an informed explanation of the technique and assessing his/her emotional state before starting.

***Example***

A client is experiencing a lot of craving, but he is unable to identify or report any relevant thoughts, feelings or precipitating situations.

*Therapist:* I would like you to try to remember the last time you experienced craving. Close your eyes and try to imagine the situation as though it is happening now.

Probe the client with the following specific questions which should be phrased in the present tense. Use these questions if necessary, that is if the client is stuck.

- Where are you?
- What time is it?
- Who is with you?
- What are you doing?
- How are you feeling?
- What thoughts are going through your mind?
- What are you telling yourself?
- What happens next?
- Can you remember any touch, taste, sounds or other senses?

This helps the client to unfold the whole experience. After the client describes the experience, the therapist explores alternative strategies using the following probes.

- What else can you do?
- What will happen then?
- How will that make you feel?

The client can be encouraged to challenge his thoughts/belief by reviewing the scenario and using the following probes

- What makes you believe that this is true?
- What else could you say to yourself?
- What is the worst thing that could happen? (Revert to downward arrow exercise).

Try to guide the client through the experience, but do not bombard him with questions. Clarify if necessary, but adhere to the client's pace. The emphasis is on reliving the experience and not answering the questions, these are just probes to facilitate the process.

***What is it useful for – topics/problems for which the technique might be used***

- Assessment (if client is not keeping daily thought record)
- Identifying and dealing with stimulus conditions
- Refusal skills/assertiveness
- Seemingly irrelevant decisions
- Problem solving
- Adapting lifestyle (changes).

***Problems – types of problems/things that go wrong and techniques/solutions*** If the client and therapist have not yet developed an effective therapeutic alliance, there is the potential for imagery to produce intense craving or powerful emotions that the client finds threatening or overwhelming. This can be avoided to some extent by clear briefing and debriefing of the client as well as allowing time at the end of the session for relaxation before leaving. Do not bombard the client, allow time to relive the experience. If emotions are very powerful or overwhelming, the client can be asked just to 'freeze' the situation and take a brief time out to recover and re-establish a sense of control. The client can be asked to hold the image but distance themselves briefly from the emotion. This can be done by asking the client to neither suppress nor engage in the experience, but just be aware that it is occurring and try and let it 'wash' over them. It is then important to re-engage with the imagery after this brief time out rather than terminating the session. If the client finds the reliving too much to bear then a less traumatic set of images could be selected before progressing. To avoid having to do this retrospectively in a session, it is good practice to use imagery in a graded practise manner or at least to establish whether this will be necessary with a particular client. That is, developing a hierarchy of images that increase in their emotional intensity so the client can work through these in a graded way. It is very important to debrief the client after using imagery techniques. This means ensuring that the client has stopped imagining the situation, and is not feeling any of the emotions or arousal evoked by the experience, that is she is not experiencing craving. Do not hesitate to double check with the client by asking directly. If they are still aroused by the experience, it might be necessary to prolong the session and reorientate them by using some alternative strategies such as relaxation and distraction (described below). If the therapist is unable to stay with the client, ensure that the client stays in the clinic until she feels well enough to leave.

***Summary of imagery***

- Useful technique for exploring real-life situations and possible outcomes, for example challenge thoughts/beliefs and imagine alternative coping strategies.
- Encourage client to relive the experience as though it is happening in the here and now.

- Can be used to help the client to look at the positive side of a drug-free lifestyle.
- Useful for clients who are not good at keeping diaries.
- Imagery can be extremely powerful, and should therefore only be used when the therapist and the client feel safe and comfortable enough to practise it.
- It is very important to debrief the client after using imagery techniques.

## Behavioural techniques

### *Activity-monitoring schedule*

Activity monitoring and scheduling can be useful basic strategies for understanding drug-and alcohol-related behaviours, and for increasing productive behaviours. This provides a picture of the client's activities, a topography of alcohol or drug use, and suggests where in the schedule activities could be changed to achieve a positive benefit. This is done by giving the client a blank grid split into the 7 days of the week, divided into 1-hour blocks. For a period of 1 week, clients record daily activities, and the degree to which they felt a sense of pleasure or mastery from participating in each activity. The client can be asked to record this on a visual analogue scale from 1 to 10.

Uses of the daily schedule are:

- Journal of present activities – gaining a basic understanding of present activities and how they relate to drug use.
- Prospective guide for future activities – can be used to schedule less drug/alcohol-related and/or more pleasurable future activities.
- Evaluation of extent to which client has been following proposed schedule successfully.
- Assessment of pleasure associated with the listed activities.

***Example***

Figure 3.4.

***What is it useful for – topics/problems for which the technique might be used***

- Assessment
- All-purpose coping plan
- Adapting lifestyle (changes)
- Boredom/emptiness.

***Problems – types of problems/things that go wrong and techniques/solutions***

This is a very basic technique, there are no particular problems associated with it

| *Time* | *Sunday* | *Monday* | *Tuesday* | *Wednesday* | *Thursday* | *Friday* | *Saturday* |
|---|---|---|---|---|---|---|---|
| *08.00* | *Asleep* | | | | | | |
| *09.00* | | | | | | | |
| *10.00* | *Breakfast* | | | | | | |
| *11.00* | *Watched* | | | | | | |
| *12.00* | *TV* | | | | | | |
| *13.00* | | | | | | | |
| *14.00* | *Lunch* | | | | | | |
| *15.00* | *Visited* | | | | | | |
| *16.00* | *Parents* | | | | | | |
| *17.00* | | | | | | | |
| *18.00* | | | | | | | |
| *19.00* | *Dinner* | | | | | | |
| *20.00* | | | | | | | |
| *21.00* | *Visited* | | | | | | |
| *22.00* | *friend* | | | | | | |
| *23.00* | | | | | | | |
| *24.00* | | | | | | | |

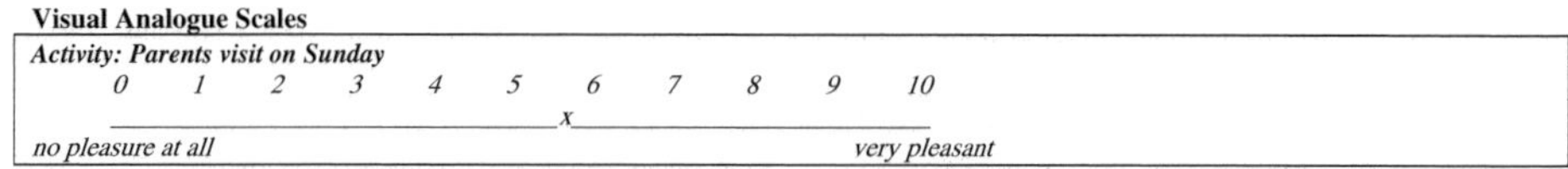


**Figure 3.4** Example of activity monitoring schedule.

other than compliance and accuracy. A possible helpful assignment would be to complete the exercise within the session for the past week starting from the previous day.

### *Relaxation training and physical exercise*

These may be encouraged by the therapist, particularly for outside the therapy session.

### *Relaxation training*

This may be a useful technique in that it provides the client with a safe (drug-free) method of relaxing. It also provides the client with a time lag after the initial craving experience during which the craving may subside. There is a number of relaxation techniques which can be used including progressive relaxation, release only relaxation, cue-controlled relaxation, differential relaxation and rapid relaxation. Relaxation techniques are also useful as they can provide a sense of control or mastery over feelings of anxiety or craving, and they can be used to challenge underlying beliefs that catastrophize physical sensations or the expectation that no improvement or change is possible. (For a detailed description of these techniques refer to Clark's chapter in Hawton *et al.*, 1995.)

#### *What is it useful for – topics/problems for which the technique might be used*

Being able to relax and feel relaxed is important, but clients may associate using drugs/alcohol with feeling relaxed. It is therefore important to explore the meaning of relaxation and address beliefs if necessary, for example getting the client to find and associate other safe (non-drug-related behaviours) with relaxation.

Some anxious clients experience discomfort when trying to relax because they feel they are losing control. This can usually be overcome by reassurance and graded practise whilst identifying the negative and extreme expectation and testing it out.

### *Physical exercise*

The therapist may encourage the client to engage in physical exercise as part of the treatment programme. This may help clients to redefine themselves as healthy, physically fit people. This image should cause cognitive dissonance for clients and may motivate them to modify the pattern of substance misuse. It may also help the client to cope with boredom, anxiety and other internal stimulus conditions. Physical exercise is also a useful distraction and breaks up negative ruminative cycles of thought. Physical exercise should be built up gradually taking into account the client's level of fitness and medical condition. Medical advice should be sought if appropriate.

### *Behavioural rehearsal (role-play and reverse role-play)*

Behavioural rehearsal is a technique which can be used in therapy as a means of illustrating any relationship problem which the client is unable to explain to the therapist or cope with. In this case, the client may take the role of the problematic other and the therapist the role of the client. It can also be used to rehearse and practise more effective/adaptive communication skills for coping with different situations, where the therapist takes the role of the problematic other person and the client can practise more effective communication techniques in a safe environment where errors can be corrected without actual consequences. The teaching component in which the therapist and client evaluate a situation and discuss more effective/adaptive responses is as important as the role-play exercise. As this technique is practised in a safe environment, it usually precedes relevant behavioural experiments. Rehearsal either through imagery (as suggested in an earlier section) or through actual behaviour is very important in acquiring new skills and coping methods. Discussion may result in the client knowing what to do, but in having very little practise in doing it. In real-life situations this may well result in failure, just as being instructed how to ride a bike is a poor substitute for the actual practise of bike riding. Practising is helpful in that it may identify previously unexpected factors, such as negative cognitions, and because physical practise will result in the acquisition of a new behaviour. With respect to the latter, overlearning is a good strategy. This is when practise during the session continues well beyond the acquisition of the new behaviour. This is on the basis that there will be some fading of the acquired skill and the real-life situation will always differ or produce unexpected challenges compared to the training situation.

#### *Example*

The client is a young woman whose closest friend is also a heavy user but not in treatment. In the past their meetings were always centred around using. In the initial stages of treatment while the client still felt very vulnerable, she was asked to avoid meeting this friend. In a role-play of this problem the therapist will be the client's friend and they role-play a scenario of the first meeting after treatment. The communication during the meeting is monitored and evaluated as they progress, and alternatives are explored and practised as appropriate.

#### *What is it useful for – topics/problems for which the technique might be used*

- Identifying and dealing with stimulus conditions
- Refusal skills/assertiveness
- All-purpose coping plan
- Seemingly irrelevant decisions
- Adapting lifestyle (changes).

#### *Problems – types of problems/things that go wrong and techniques/solutions*

Role-play is artificial and it may be difficult to portray a real situation. It is therefore important for the therapist to check regularly with the client to clarify that the role-play closely resembles the real situation. Rehearsing the role-play in imagination can be a useful way of preparing or priming the client to the actual experience. Role-play can also arouse intense emotions in some people. As in the case of guided imagery, plenty of time should be allowed at the end of the session to allow the client to be debriefed and recover before going home. Also the intensity of role-play will depend on the quality of the therapeutic relationship with the client.

#### *Summary of behavioural rehearsal and role-play*

- Used in therapy to illustrate relationship problems which the client is unable to explain
- Used to rehearse and practise effective/adaptive communication skills for coping with different situations in a safe environment where errors can be corrected without consequences
- Teaching component is as important as the role-play
- Therapist should check regularly with client to clarify that role-play closely resembles reality
- Role-play can arouse intense emotions so allow time for client to be debriefed.

### *Behavioural experiments*

Behavioural experiments are used to test clients' ability to challenge their drug- or alcohol-related beliefs and core beliefs, and to practise newly learned adaptive coping skills. The essence of this technique is that it is an experiment used to test whether a specified belief is true or not. It is based upon the assumption that clients hold beliefs or expectations that are not true, but due to biases in thinking (such as selectively attending to certain information or events rather than others), or the use of avoidant or safety behaviour (so that the belief is reinforced or not shown to be incorrect), these inappropriate beliefs are strengthened and fail to be challenged. A behavioural experiment involves manipulating a situation so that an incorrect or inappropriate belief is challenged and disproved. An inappropriate belief is identified and the client encouraged to specify what will occur in a particular situation should that belief turn out to be true and to predict what would happen if it turns out to be untrue. The experiment is a behavioural test of two competing hypotheses generated from the client's inappropriate belief. The client is then encouraged to carry out the experiment, to observe what happens and to draw appropriate conclusions. Initially the client will most likely need considerable help through prompts from the therapist but the exercise should be repeated until the client is able to independently generate ways of testing out beliefs.

Behavioural experiments are particularly useful when there is an affective response and an associated change in behaviour. For example: when anxiety is associated with avoidance. This almost always indicates that there is some type of catastrophic thinking or anticipation present that can be tested out through asking clients to change their behaviour.

For a more detailed description of using behavioural experiments in clinical practice see Bennett-Levy *et al.* (2004).

Behavioural experiments can be carried out in two ways:

1. In real circumstances: for example, a client may have a belief such as, 'I am unable to refuse drugs', and will be asked to expose himself to a drug stimulus such as walking past the dealer's house. They can be assisted by the use of the techniques which they have rehearsed for coping with these situations. The client is therefore able to test himself by challenging his core and drug-related beliefs in a situation in which he is vulnerable, and therefore increase his self-efficacy. Behavioural experiments can be used to test out the reality and validity of any maladaptive thoughts. In this way the thought can be identified and isolated from any emotional connection, by for example simply writing down the thought. The client, prompted by the therapist, can make various predictions that follow on from that thought. These predictions are usually extreme and/or catastrophic, such as 'I will always fail' or 'If I do that I'll go mad'. The therapist aims to build on these extreme predictions and assist the client in experimenting so that the prediction is disproved and shown to be incorrect.
2. 'As if' technique: the therapist asks the client to imagine that she is in a desirable situation, for example not using and employed, and act as if a desired set of circumstances were true for her. This activity can be used to help modify behaviour and lifestyle. The 'as if' technique should be used as a staged rehearsal for an actual test or when it is impractical to be exposed to the real situation.

***Example***

Using the previous example, as treatment progresses and the client feels more confident, the client may be asked to arrange a meeting with her friend firstly in a protected environment, with support if necessary, and gradually moving to more real circumstances. If the meeting does not go well, this is a good opportunity for the therapist to explore the meaning of the friendship.

### *What is it useful for – topics/problems for which the technique might be used*

- Identifying and dealing with stimulus conditions
- Refusal skills/assertiveness
- All-purpose coping plan
- Seemingly irrelevant decisions
- Problem solving
- Adapting lifestyle (changes).

### *Problems – types of problems/things that go wrong and techniques/solutions*

Experiments to test out inappropriate beliefs can be used at any time during treatment but they should become increasingly more powerful and effective as treatment progresses. Behavioural experiments that involve exposure to real-life drug using or drinking situations should be carried out later in the treatment, when other techniques have been rehearsed and consolidated and the client feels confident enough. Exposure should be graded, that is ask the client to rate situations for vulnerability, and start with the least difficult. Each level should be consolidated before moving on to the next. If the experiment is not successful, that is the client relapses, the therapist must encourage the client to continue with treatment and learn from the experience by evaluating the event to examine what went wrong.

Frequently a number of behavioural experiments need to be carried out to produce lasting cognitive change. Clients will often engage in 'hypothesis protection', that is they will ignore evidence contrary to their beliefs, and selectively attend to supportive evidence. When this cognitive bias occurs, it can be pointed out and used as a helpful example of selective attention. Therefore, it is usually necessary to carry out numerous behavioural experiments and constantly refer to their results, so that the overwhelming evidence supports a rational viewpoint and challenges the client's beliefs. Clients can also engage in the 'Yes, but...' argument against the evidence and conclusions resulting from a behavioural experiment. Again, this can be pointed out and the client taught self-instructions to focus on the salient aspect of the experiment.

### *Summary of behavioural experiments*

- Test the client's ability to challenge drug/core beliefs
- Practise newly learned adaptive coping skills
- Behavioural experiments can be carried out in real circumstances or imaginary 'as if' technique
- Should not be carried out until later in treatment when other techniques have been rehearsed and consolidated and client feels confident enough

- Exposure should be graded
- Each level should be consolidated before moving on to the next.

### *Contingency management*

Contingency management (CM), also known as 'incentive, positive reinforcement approaches', is a technique based on operant conditioning principles whereby clients are rewarded for particular behaviours, for example drug-free urine tests, attendance to groups. The aim of CM is to facilitate behavioural change and by providing clear and attainable behavioural goals for the client (Griffith, Rowan-Szal, Roark and Simpson, 2000). This can be achieved by adhering to operant learning principles, for example, the timing of rewards and aiming rewards at reducing one type of behaviour, such as reducing intake of one drug rather than several (Griffith *et al.*, 2000). Whilst there is no specific model of CM, there are four general principles to guide its application in a therapeutic setting: (i) regular assessment or testing is necessary in order to ensure that the client is adhering to the treatment programme; (ii) the client and therapist agree that rewards will not be given if the client fails to follow the treatment plan; (iii) the client and therapist work together to develop suitable alternative activities for the client; (iv) the giving and withholding of rewards must be consistent (Higgins and Petry, 1999).

The therapist and client will discuss the methods of reward most suitable to the individual, this is something that may need to be explored in some detail so that a workable system can be set up. If other staff or family members are involved, it must be ensured that they all understand how it works. A reward should be given consistently and immediately on successful 'completion' of a reward task, for example drug-free urine, attendance to a session. Depending on the nature of the reward, some 'immediate awards' may need to be a certificate stating that the client has earned a reward which will be received later. Rewards should be increased over the course of the treatment in line with the number of consecutive successful tasks completed. If the client fails on a 'reward task', then the reinforcement schedule must be reset. With continued consecutive success, the schedule can be gradually phased out over the course of the treatment. It is hoped that by the time the CM schedule is being phased out, the client will be starting to feel the benefits of the treatment, and these in themselves will be rewards.

Types of reward task may include:

- Drug-free urine tests
- Attendance to sessions and appointments
- Useful contributions to session and appointments
- Effort displayed in organizing issues which would arise on completion of in-patient treatment (housing, work, education, training, personal relationships). This would differ between clients and would need to be determined in the initial meeting.

Types of reward may include:

- Book vouchers
- Cinema vouchers
- Food vouchers
- Clothes vouchers
- Transport vouchers.

***What is it useful for – topics/problems for which the technique might be used*** This technique should be used throughout the therapy but particularly the following:

- Identifying and dealing with stimulus conditions
- Craving
- Seemingly irrelevant decisions
- Adapting lifestyle (changes).

***Problems – types of problems/things that go wrong and techniques/solutions*** A number of problems can be encountered with this technique, so it requires careful planning and a full understanding of the theoretical premise upon which it is based, that is, operant conditioning. Some common problems which have been identified include the following:

- Rewarding only one behaviour may not treat the client as a whole and therefore would not impact on behaviour other than the specific behavioural target of the reward.
- Developing a reward schedule that will work for the client, that is the rewards need to be attractive enough for the client to want to receive them, and at the same time not too costly to the service. Cost has been found to be one of the drawbacks of this technique.
- A poor or incomplete understanding of the technique and its application in this context will not be effective.
- Whilst it might be useful in the early stages of treatment as a means of helping clients who have difficulty with maintaining motivation and taking responsibility, it is a mistake to make it a permanent 'crutch' or 'prop' upon which the client becomes too dependent. The ultimate aim should be for clients to develop enough of a sense of self and responsibility for their lives to be able to make decisions about using without relying upon schedules which provide rewards which cannot be part of everyday life.

***Summary of contingency management*** CM is based on operant conditioning principles and the aim of CM is to facilitate behavioural change by providing clear and attainable behavioural goals for the client.

There are four general principles of CM:

**(i)** Regular assessment/testing to ensure adherence to treatment programme.

**(ii)** Client and therapist agree that rewards will not be given if treatment plan is not adhered to.

**(iii)** Client and therapist work together to develop suitable alternative activities for the client.

**(iv)** Giving and withholding of rewards must be consistent.

CHAPTER FOUR

# Agenda setting and structure of sessions

## Treatment sessions

### *Topic and session*

To start with we need to clarify the difference between 'topics' and 'sessions' as they are used in this book. A 'topic' refers to the theme to be covered in a session. The topics are divided into core and elective. Ideally, one topic should be covered in each session, at least at the initial stages of treatment. A session refers to the clinical session in which the topics will be covered. Sessions have three parts. The topic or topics are covered in the second, or in other words, the main part of the session. All clients will cover the topics included under the core topics heading. This is because core topics address concepts which are considered to be fundamental to the CBT theory of addiction, or problems which are relevant to all clients, independently of substances used. However, the number of sessions devoted to each topic, and the order of topics may vary according to the needs of clients, so this should be based on assessment and formulation. The same can be said for the number and range of elective topics. The elective topics allow for other problem areas to be addressed within the treatment programme in order to allow for flexibility in meeting individual needs. Elective topics may be incorporated into the treatment programme as required, and need not necessarily be kept until all of the core topics have been covered. It is, however, advisable for less experienced therapists to follow the order of core topics as suggested in the book (with flexibility on the number of sessions allocated per topic). Elective topics can then be added if appropriate (again with flexibility on the number of sessions allocated per topic) before the relapse prevention topic and the termination topic. In this way, there is balance between structure, focus and flexibility of the treatment offered.

For example, it is logical to start treatment with topic 1 (identifying stimulus conditions) because there is a specific decision-making process for each stimulus condition. Some are easy to identify, but others may be more difficult. The next topic should be 'coping with stimulus conditions' and this should be followed by 'coping with craving'. If a client has a particular difficulty with refusing offers of drugs, then 'assertiveness training' might need to be added here rather than after 'seemingly irrelevant decisions'. If a client presents with automatized behaviour, then emphasis should be on the initial topics of 'identifying stimulus conditions', 'seemingly irrelevant decisions', 'coping with craving' before moving on to other topics such as 'assertiveness training' among others.

### *Number of sessions*

There is no specific number of sessions required, or in other words there is no recommended number of sessions proven to be related to positive outcome. It makes sense that each patient should receive at least 12 sessions (two assessment sessions and nine core topic sessions) of 50 minutes in an individual treatment setting. However, this is something that should be based upon the individual's specific needs. Therapists should not feel under pressure to restrict the number of sessions offered. It is usually extremely difficult to predict how easy it will be to cover the core topics. Revision of case formulation is often necessary in order to incorporate new information elicited during treatment and use skills gained so far.

### *Duration of session*

Fifty minutes is the typical duration of an individual session. Longer sessions might be exhausting for both client and therapist. Shorter sessions might be inadequate to cover topics in detail. If the client has to leave early, the length of the session should be agreed if possible at the beginning, so that the structure can be adhered to. If the duration is not enough to cover a topic then further sessions should be allocated to that topic, or the topic should be revisited later. Fifty minutes also allows for the therapist to use 10 minutes before or after the session to prepare or make notes. If the client is late and there is little time left, the session should still be divided into three parts. In the second part, instead of covering the scheduled topic, client and therapist can discuss issues related to the late arrival of the client. The therapist should remember to use every opportunity to enhance the client's motivation to change, and reinforce the need to take responsibility for actions. Arriving late or cancelling the session may be associated with the client's ambivalence about treatment, and could be part of a lifestyle that the individual considers he/she has little or no control over. In any case, the therapist should remember to explore the meaning of the event, and help clients to learn from their decisions and actions. Concepts such as 'denial' are problematic because they have a pessimistic connotation, and because they are static. In the CBT approach, the above issues are seen as challenges that are connected with ambivalence, and therefore need to be incorporated and addressed in treatment.

## Treatment structure

### *The importance of structure*

Each session is divided into three parts. The second part, usually the longer one, is the main part of the session, in which the main topic will be discussed. The first and third parts of the session are the same for all sessions. The session structure should be adhered to even if the same topic is covered in more than one session. It should also be adhered to during assessment sessions and in the termination session. Structure is important, not to provide an ordered session, but to develop and maintain a collaborative component in the treatment. It allows for the following:

- Best use of allocated time.
- Shared responsibility of the use of the time.
- It helps clients to experience what structure feels like during the session and then practise it in their life.
- It acknowledges the importance of out-of-session assignments (first and third part).
- It emphasizes the importance of setting a collaborative agenda for every session.
- It emphasizes control, prediction and planning, and therefore reduces automatized behaviours and cognitive distortions which can be influenced by negative emotions.

Structure itself is not the aim of therapy, but the means with which to achieve collaboration and to maintain focus. Structuring the session might feel somehow artificial and imposed. It might make the therapist feel uncomfortable. In particular less experienced therapists might feel under pressure to structure and adhere to the topic allocated, thus making the whole therapy process very mechanical. Is the concept of structure something really new to the clinical practice? If we take a moment to reflect, we will see that clinicians usually have a structure in mind and a plan of what should be covered in a clinical meeting. In any type of consultation (medical, psychological, a simple keyworking session, even the very short ones), clinicians enter the session with a plan of how to use the time. What is new about the CBT model is that the structure is stable, overt and shared with the client. The structure is even linked with setting an agenda for the session, which is essential for developing and maintaining a collaborative approach. It is crucial for the therapist to first understand the importance and the necessity of structure, and secondly to discuss this with the client, either during the assessment sessions, or at the beginning of every session if appropriate.

### *How to structure the session*

We recommend that each session should be divided into three parts. In a typical 50-minute session the division should be as follows:

- First part – 15 minutes
- Second part – 20 minutes/main part of the session
- Third part – 15 minutes.

If the session is longer (i.e. 60 minutes) then it should be divided into equal parts.

### First part

***Introduction of session format*** After welcoming and making the client feel at ease, the therapist introduces the session by agreeing to the duration of the session, and reminding the client about the structure and format of the session. If this is the first assessment session, or there has been a break for a period of time, this introduction is very important. The initial part of the interaction with the client is crucial for setting up a collaborative climate.

***Example***

Therapist: 'As this is our first meeting, I think it is very important to discuss and agree on how we are going to use our time overall, and in each of our meetings. In CBT, we are very keen to have a structure during the sessions. It is, however, even more important to talk and agree on this, and to try our best to adhere to this structure'.

It is also important to explain to the client why structure is important and make sure that the client is in agreement. It is important to keep in mind that clients might have experienced different therapeutic approaches, and therefore the concept of structure in therapy might be somewhat alien to them. If the client is resistant to this concept, and/or to the concept of having a mutually agreed agenda, then it is advisable to agree to follow the structure and to review the client's experience at the end of the session. It might also be important to explore early in the treatment what structure means to the client, and to try to de-catastrophize any erroneous assumptions around the therapist imposing topics and format of sessions.

With time, the introduction about the format of the sessions can become very simple, that is as you recall, we divide our time into three parts.

***Review of life events since last sessions*** The therapist and client briefly review life issues since the last session, for example episodes of use, craving and family issues. This review should be very brief or even epigrammatic and become the bridge for the next step.

***Elicit current concerns/problems*** This is essential to maintain and reinforce the collaboration between the client and therapist, so that the client feels that the therapist is addressing any problems in the course of the therapy. It may determine what is going to be covered in the session, that is in the case of a new problem, or if a crisis situation arises.

***Review of previous sessions*** The therapist and client briefly review the topics covered in the previous sessions and remind themselves of what was agreed for the current session. In this way, the concept of continuity and the importance of achieving small steps at the time are emphasized. The client therefore feels part of and in control of the therapy process, and builds on the mutual trust and shared responsibility.

***Review of out-of-session assignments*** This may take the form of reviewing a diary, or some other out-of-session assignment that has been allocated for that week. If the client has carried out an out-of-session assignment, it should be reviewed and evaluated, otherwise it will not have a purpose from the client's point of view. Out-of-session assignments should be rewarded, as it is a way to modify dysfunctional beliefs and behaviours, and explore and develop new ways of coping. Encourage out-of-session practise, but do not criticize or become judgemental if it has not happened. At the end of the day, non-adherence might reflect the therapist's difficulty in explaining clearly what practise is about, inability to allocate appropriate practise, or it may just be a reflection of the chaotic lifestyle of the client and therefore be premature to expect adherence at this point. The review should be brief and if major issues are identified, then therapist and client collaboratively might want to expand on those issues in the main part of the session (include it in the agenda for the session).

***Agree the agenda for the session*** It is now appropriate to agree on the topic to be covered in the session (or sometimes topics). If all previous steps were covered appropriately (though briefly), agenda setting should follow naturally. Do not jump to conclusions or rush to follow what you have in your mind. The therapy process is a live and collaborative process. What theory says is important, and what was agreed following the case formulation is also important, but what is most important is what the client brings to the session. The meaning the client attributes to what is happening in their life and the treatment process itself. Formulation is a hypothesis and as such can be revisited and modified.

***Example***

Therapist: 'What do you think should we cover today? Should we cover what was agreed before, or should we explore further what happened this week between you and your girlfriend?'

It might be appropriate to stay with the same topic, and use the out-of-session assigments to consolidate what client achieved.

### Main part

This part of the session is the one described in detail under the separate topic headings in the next two chapters (core and elective topics). We should emphasize once more the importance of continuity of treatment and the concordance of topics discussed in the case formulation. This means the ongoing process of reformulation on one hand, and the importance of making sessions relevant to the problems and issues that the client brings to the therapy on the other.

### Third part

This is the part of the session that it is crucial to have adequate time to complete. If all previous steps were done properly, there should be enough time to summarize and prepare for the week to come. If the agenda was not collaborative, this is when the consequences will become clear. The usual signs are: (i) the client brings new major issues towards the very end of the session, leaving no time to address them; (ii) the new issues are so fundamental that the session seems now irrelevant or false; (iii) the client is passive, unable to summarize or provide feedback, which makes the therapist feel that they were preaching or teaching rather than working with the client. This is why such an emphasis is placed on structuring the session and developing a mutual agreed agenda for the session.

***Elicit client's views*** Do not hesitate to ask for feedback about what has been discussed in the main part. If there are any of the above signs of noncollaboration, address them at this point. There are still 15 minutes remaining to build on collaboration and to enhance motivation. Encourage honest feedback. Propose to explore the issue further next time. Allocate assignments which are relevant to how to collaborate. Remember to acknowledge responsibility for what went wrong in the session. Don't forget therapy itself is a learning process for both client and therapist.

***Out-of-session assignments for the coming week*** Out-of-session assignments are a very important part of the treatment. In order to encourage the clients to practise, they must be able to understand why it is important. It is also important for the client to have written instructions and to make a note of the agreed out-of-session assignment. If the out-of-session assignment has not already been discussed in the session, time should be kept to practise the assignment and ensure that the client understands what is expected and the purpose of the assignment. If the client has reading/writing difficulties, a nonwritten format of the assignment should be agreed and practised with the client. This means that the format of the out-of-session assignment might be slightly different.

The following are some basic principles about out-of-session assignments:

- Be clear with your instructions
- Be specific
- Be economical and prioritize what is important and what is not
- Do not allocate to much
- Make clear links with the session.

Remember the best assignment is the one that is proposed and undertaken by the client, the therapist is only there to facilitate review and learning from it; therefore stay back and give the initiative to the client.

***Summary*** This is the last chance that the therapist and client have within the session to ensure that all important issues identified have been covered, and that the client understands what has been covered in the session. This can be achieved by either the client or the therapist summarizing the content and main points of the session. If the therapist is summarizing, as will probably be the case in the early sessions, it is important that the therapist confirms that the client is in agreement with the summary.

## Summary of treatment sessions and treatment structure

- All clients should cover all core topics.
- Number of sessions devoted to each topic and order of topics may vary with client needs.
- Number and range of elective topics will vary according to client needs.
- Client should receive at least twelve 50-minute sessions and session structure should be adhered to.
- Sessions have three parts:

  - first part includes introduction of session format, review of life events, review of previous sessions and out-of-session assignment, elicitation of current concerns/problems, setting of the agenda
  - second part is the main part, where the topic will be covered
  - third part includes elicitation of client's views, allocation of out-of-session assignment and summary of the session.

CHAPTER FIVE

# Assessment and case formulation

## Introduction

As in every professional interaction (medical, psychological or other), the beginning and most crucial step of interaction/treatment is a thorough assessment. In the UK treatment system, the client is taken through a number of different assessments on the treatment pathway. Each has a different aim, but all should share one common aim: to enhance the client's motivation to engage in and remain in treatment. In the CBT model presented in this book, motivational enhancement techniques and strategies are used throughout treatment (e.g. Socratic questioning, rolling with resistance), and should be considered to be a therapy technique rather than a different therapeutic approach incorporated into the CBT model. There is also an additional core topic dedicated to motivational enhancement that can be used either to start treatment, or later when necessary.

Models of care introduce three essential stages of assessment or information gathering: screening, triage assessment and comprehensive assessment. The CBT assessment will follow the comprehensive assessment that the client will receive within the treatment modality that the therapy is offered. Therefore, some aspects of the history and current drug use, as well as physical and psychosocial complications/consequences would have been already discussed and documented. In view of this, unnecessary repetition should be avoided. It is important that the aim of the assessment is clear to the therapist and subsequently explained to the client. It is also important to formulate information gathered in the assessment and use it in a way that will be useful in the therapeutic process. This is particularly important when the client's key worker is the one providing the CBT. A simple introduction is useful.

***Example***

'In every new treatment, it is important to start with an assessment of the problem. I am aware that you have already met several of my colleagues, and you may have already discussed several points which we will cover today too. However, it is important for both of us to review these points and understand them from a cognitive-behavioural perspective'.

It might be also helpful to proceed with a general introduction to the CB theory.

***Example***

'In CBT we try to explore and understand not what happened, but what the event means. For example...'

'According to CB theory, people drink alcohol because they expect that alcohol will benefit them in a positive way. In the same way, people consider or try to stop when they think that something bad will happen if they continue drinking, and when they feel strong enough to get on with their lives without drinking. With this in mind, let's try to understand what drinking means to you'. or 'How can we understand your drinking pattern'.

It is important to adhere to the session structure as presented in the previous chapter, therefore this also needs to be explained to the client. The collaborative nature of the therapy and the shared responsibility also need to be emphasized. The session topics presented next in this chapter should be covered during the main part of the session (see Chapter 4).

The assessment format presented here incorporates aspects of the assessment process of Beck *et al.* (1993) (developmental profile and case formulation), Carroll (1998) (functional analysis) and Miller and Rollnick (1991) (motivational strategies). It is divided into two topics with an optional third topic, and it will take a minimum of two sessions with an additional optional third session. In cognitive-behaviour therapy, the assessment is not just an information-gathering exercise, it is also an important part of the therapeutic process in which the therapist enables clients to start understanding their substance misuse behaviour.

***Summary of assessment***

Assessment topic 1

Functional analysis of current pattern of use and associated problems
Reasons for seeking treatment

Assessment topic 2

Developmental profile, substance use history and treatment history
First attempt at case formulation

Optional separate assessment topic 3

Presentation of and education in the cognitive model
Review of case formulation
Negotiation of treatment goals and rules of therapy
Get ready to start therapy

## ▶ Assessment topic 1

***Current pattern of drug use and associated lifestyle problems***

In the first assessment session, the aim is to explore in detail the client's drinking or drug-taking behaviour. You can use information from previous assessments, but you need: (i) specific details of drinking/drug taking in order to reconstruct the exact process of use (functional analysis); (ii) to incorporate and understand this information using the cognitive model (i.e. stimulus conditions, beliefs, actions); (iii) to assess whether there is any automatized behaviour; (iv) to explore where to put the emphasis in the treatment programme, and in what order to offer the topics; and finally, (v) to know the client's strong or weak points as far as a cognitive-behavioural understanding of the problem is concerned.

Here we remind you of some aspects of the client's current pattern of substance use and lifestyle problems that should be covered. Although the following aspects may seem basic for an experienced clinician, there are at times some details which can be crucial:

- What substances are used and how they are related?
  Ensure that you have assessed the use of all substances, including alcohol and prescribed medication. Focus on the relationship between the use of different substances. This is particularly important in the case of multiple substance use. We have already discussed in detail how to use the model with this group of clients. Remember that details of the exact type of drink and substances used are important.
- How are the substances used (frequency, quantity, route of use)?
  The frequency of use might be related to the lifestyle of the individual, aspects of family life, work and personality, and might of course be triggers as well as seemingly irrelevant decisions for further substance use.
- Social circumstances of substance use (place, other people involved).
  In the same way, place of use can be related to the above.
- Source of drug supply (dealer, practical problems to get supply, emotional issues).
  Issues around the source of drug supply can give you a lot of information and ideas about how to develop a strategy to delay the process of action involved in acquiring drugs, and break the circle of automatized behaviour. Some clients might have a special relationship with their dealers. There may also be other issues related to alcohol or prescribed drugs, such as opening times of the corner shop.
- Family support or other issues
  Presence of other users or drinkers in the family should always be assessed. This can have a major impact at several points in the model, such as stimulus conditions, confidence and lifestyle changes. The impact of family members can be dual. It can be positive: they can increase motivation, reinforce implementation of coping strategies or support behavioural experiments. It can also be negative in that it can put pressure on the individual without allowing him to take responsibility for his actions, and adverse emotional states with family members can be stimulus conditions for use.
- Employment issues and financial consequences.
  Employment can have a very important stabilizing effect on a client's life, but it can also have negative effect: payment day can be a stimulus condition for use,

so the focus of early coping strategies might be on control of finances or lifestyle changes.

- Medical problems and psychological problems
  Presence of medical problems can motivate people to change and improve lifestyle and quality of life, but they can also facilitate further use because of the client's cognitive distortions in processing the health-related information. For example, the client can catastrophize: 'I am going to die anyway'. There is a similar risk with psychological issues related to substance misuse. Depression or anxiety states can affect the client's thinking process: 'there is no escape from this', or 'I can't do it'. Detailed assessment of psychological issues is very important. This model can be flexible with the use of elective topics to address psychological and other issues (see Chapter 7).
- Legal problems
  Assessment of legal problems is important for several reasons: (i) to give an indication of how motivated the client is (this doesn't mean that clients who are on probation or a court treatment order can't change or benefit from treatment); (ii) issues such as collaboration, confidentiality or continuity of treatment can be affected; (iii) liaison with other professionals is crucial to avoid giving clients conflicting messages (the therapy process does not take place in a vacuum); (iv) as with all other aspects of current substance use mentioned above, the presence of legal problems can have a dual role: they can motivate the client to engage in treatment and change and/or make the client suspicious or defensive.

To summarize, it is important to remember to avoid making assumptions about the meaning of the above-mentioned aspects of current use. It is also important to remember that the same issue can have conflicting meanings. For example, work can give stability, but also provide the means for ongoing use. The therapist must avoid judgements of whether an interpretation is appropriate or not. Some clients have a tendency to give answers that will satisfy the therapist and be acceptable to society. The first assessment session it is very important as it can show to the client that the therapist is open minded, nonjudgemental and prefers a collaborative approach in therapy.

### *Functional analysis*

***What is it?*** We have already discussed the importance of gathering detailed information with the aim of reconstructing the process of use, and to help the client to start understanding his own behaviour and the decision-making process involved, to enable him to take control.

Functional analysis means identifying the client's thoughts, feelings and circumstances, before and after substance use, and it is essentially the same as the technique described in the daily thought record. It is like zooming in on the action and slowing down the motion to study the details as in a replay of action in a film. Functional analysis will be the first exposure of the client of what CBT is about. Later on, functional analysis will be used in several topics, such as the identifying stimulus conditions and seemingly irrelevant decisions (usually the first topics in therapy). Drink and drug diaries are often used in everyday clinical practice as a means of gathering information about a client's substance using behaviour; in particular the pattern of use, quantity and routes of use. Functional analysis is very similar to drink and drug diaries, with the difference being making links between this information and the CBT model that emphasizes the importance of decision making. It is detailed and it is functional with the aim of facilitating an understanding of how the two are related.

***How to do it*** Functional analysis is a very simple process of reconstruction. So far you have gathered detailed information about client's use: when it takes place, how (buying, using techniques, place of use) and what happens afterwards. Now, using typical examples or examples of more recent use, do the functional analysis. It is necessary to help the client to remember in detail the episode of use, and from this point of view, functional analysis follows the same steps as an imagery technique.

The basic steps involved are: antecedent (where, when, with whom); behaviour (what, how); consequences (emotional, behavioural and social) (known as ABC schedules). Using this very basic skeleton of functional analysis, you can add other aspects such as thoughts before use, craving experiences and positive and negative consequences of use. In this way functional analysis can be linked with the CBT model, the cognitive and behavioural techniques, and between-session practice (see figure 5.1).

Clients may have typical patterns of use and/or use in a very unpredictable way. In this session, you invite and help the client to describe (as if seen in a video), the process of use.

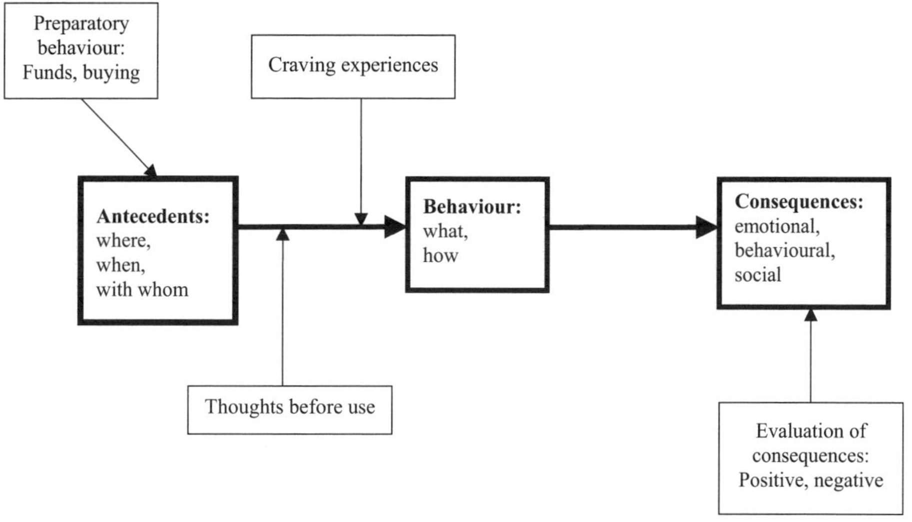


**Figure 5.1** Functional analysis.

It is important to make several attempts at functional analysis within the session. Practice this exercise with the client for at least three different recent episodes of use.

### *Example of questioning process for functional analysis*

- Tell me all you can about the last time you used heroin?
- Where were you?
- What were you doing?
- What happened before?
- What thoughts came into your mind?
- How were you feeling?
- When was the first time you were aware of wanting to use?
- What was the high like at the beginning and what was it like later?
- Can you think of anything positive that happened as a result of using?
- What about the negative consequences?

### *Reasons for seeking treatment*

It is very common practice and part of the initial screening, as well as the triage assessment procedure, to ask clients about the reasons why they are seeking treatment at this point of their lives. This information is crucial for several reasons: (i) it reflects the client's motivational stage (see chapter 3); (ii) it sheds light on the client's belief system (positive and negative expectancies) in relation to substance use; (iii) it encourages clients to take responsibility for their treatment, because treatment is presented as a choice (even in the case of criminal justice system treatment interventions). This is a delicate question, it should be asked in a nonjudgemental way, because it can easily be misinterpreted by clients that the therapist is pessimistic about the outcome of treatment.

The therapist should also be aware (as with the advantages/disadvantages analysis, and the identification and challenging of positive and negative outcome expectancies) that: (i) the client might try to keep the therapist happy by responding with what 'he thinks is considered to be' the right answer; (ii) the client might not express his own views but those of the family, friends and/or other users; (iii) the reasons given may contradict each other. This contradiction does not mean that the client is lying. It is often and sometimes desirable that the client holds conflicting views/beliefs, because this can be the starting point for cognitive modification (challenging beliefs).

### *Out-of-session practice assignment*

Ask the client to keep either a daily thought record or activity-monitoring schedule for the forthcoming week. The complexity of the above practices will depend on:

(i) how successfully you have completed the examples of functional analysis within the session; (ii) the client's ability to contribute to it; and (iii) the presence of automatized behaviour. Use simple diaries or basic ABC monitoring schedules if necessary. Use the same columns that you have used during the session, and if you add any other aspect of the CBT model make sure that your client is confident and clear about what is expected. Remember that out-of-session practise is crucial to the success of treatment, but you need to find the right balance between the client taking active responsibility of his treatment on the one hand, and maintaining the therapeutic alliance on the other, by avoiding creating performance anxiety or making the client feel patronized or undermined.

## Assessment topic 2

### *Substance use history and developmental profile*

As with the first assessment topic on current use and associated lifestyle problems, it is very likely that the information required on substance use history and developmental profile might be available, as it would have been acquired through the other assessments. The aim of this topic is to bring together the information available about: (i) previous use; (ii) early development; and (iii) more specific information about cognitive and emotional development. Using this information, a clinical hypothesis based on cognitive-behavioural theory will be created (see Chapter 2).

This clinical hypothesis is called case formulation, and should include early experiences that contributed to the development and maintenance of core beliefs.

The developmental profile should include relevant information from social history, educational history, medical history, psychiatric history, vocational history, family (genetic predisposition) and relationship history, personality development and significant life events. These experiences may not necessarily be traumatic, however, messages that children receive about themselves form the foundation of their beliefs about themselves. This information, in conjunction with personality characteristics and genetic predisposition, may have an impact on the development of substance use problems in later life. The emphasis should be on experiences relevant to the development of substance misuse such as:

- How did the client function prior to using drugs or drinking alcohol? Focus on positive and negative aspects?
- How did the client start using or drinking?
- How did initial use lead to abuse and dependence (if present)?
- What has prevented the client from being able to stop the substance use?
- How did key beliefs develop? (core and substance-related beliefs)—see relevant section.

### *Treatment history*

For the therapist the focus of the assessment should be to get to know the client and establish a relationship of trust. Exploration of the reasons for seeking treatment, as well as treatment history can play an important role at this point. Special emphasis should be placed on identifying factors that contributed to previous treatment success and abstinence periods. This can be achieved through a series of open-ended questions. Treatment history can also enhance motivation to engage in treatment, and change current behaviour. Treatment history can help the client to learn from previous treatment attempts, de-catastrophize any failures, and therefore improve self-confidence.

### *Example*

- Have you received any treatment for opiate misuse before? When was that? Can you tell me a little more about it? What did you like or not like about the programme? What do you think made you stop attending?
- Have you ever received any treatment for misuse of other substances? (Repeat as for the question above).
- Have you had any periods of abstinence? When was the last one? Can you tell me a little bit more about that period? What do you think helped you to maintain that abstinence?
- Have you had any periods of abstinence in the last 3 months? Can you tell me more about that – how did that start and end?
- Everyone has good and bad points, what do you think are your particular 'good' and 'bad' points with regard to how you are coping?

### *Case formulation*

The case formulation is the first attempt to make sense of the individual's life in the context of the CBT model. Although we suggest that the assessment should start with the current problem and move to the substance use history and developmental profile, the order of the case formulation should be chronological. This involves integrating the information (developmental profile and functional analysis) obtained in the assessment sessions so far, into a 'story of the client's life'. The developmental profile and the functional analysis are the basis of the case formulation. This is where the therapist and client piece together the information to represent the client's problem using the cognitive theory and model. Case formulation can be divided into two parts (see figure 5.2):

i. The first part represents the client's early experiences and development of core beliefs (about him/herself, the world and the future), development of substance use problem/related beliefs, and compensatory strategies. This part of the formulation is generic.

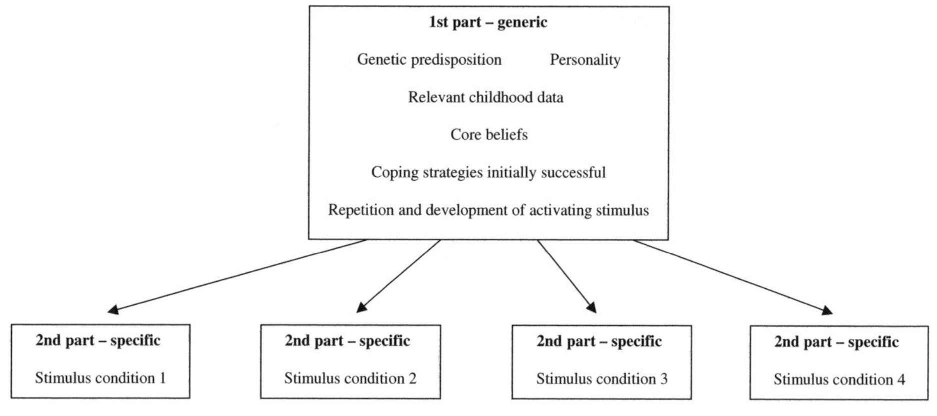


**Figure 5.2** Model of case formulation.



ii. The second part represents the functional analysis, which is an analysis of situations encountered currently, and it is specific, therefore different formulations should be developed for the different situations encountered. The response to these situations is influenced by early experiences, core beliefs and of course drug-related beliefs.

We have already mentioned that the case formulation is a clinical hypothesis, based on the available information at this point of treatment which might need to be modified at a later stage when more information is available (with the treatment progress and development of the therapeutic alliance). It is crucial, however, in order to start treatment based on theory and a specific model, to develop a case formulation at the end of the assessment process, and share it with the client. It is of paramount importance that the case formulation is a collaborative approach; the client brings personal experience and information, and the therapist knowledge of the CBT model that will be used in treatment.

For new therapists who have limited experience of developing a case formulation, discussing the information gathered during supervision before presenting and discussing the formulation with the client might be helpful. If you are uncertain about the case formulation that you have in mind remember the following two points:

i. The best person to discuss the case formulation with and share your thoughts about it, is the actual client.

ii. Collaboration is the cornerstone of CBT. Therefore a shared case formulation which is incomplete is better and more productive, than an excellent case formulation imposed and not shared with the client.

***Example***

See Figure 5.3.

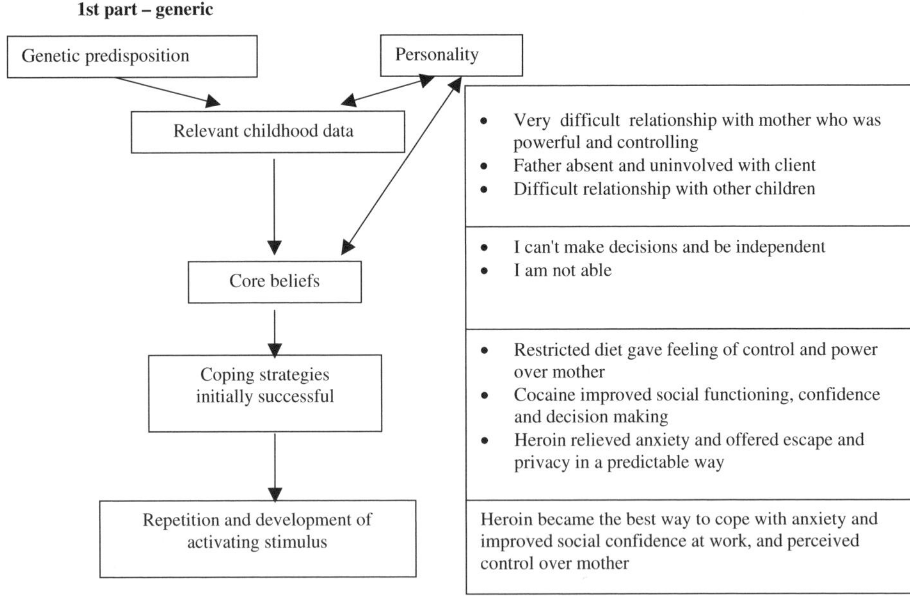


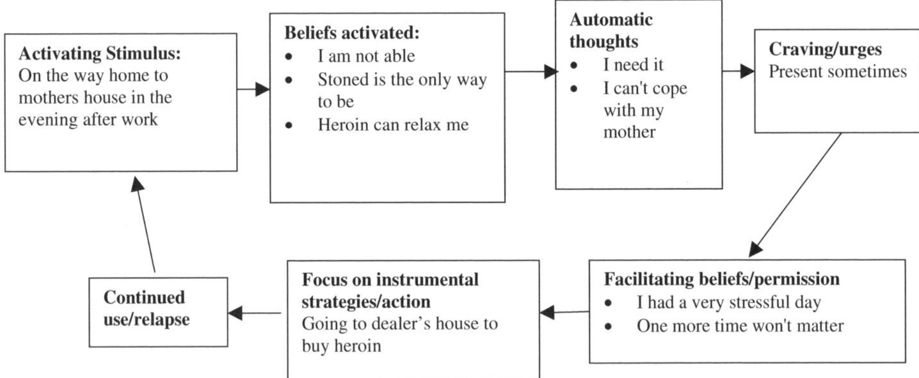


**Figure 5.3** Example of case formulation.

## Optional assessment topic 3

This paragraph describes an optional third assessment topic. It is optional in the sense that the items included can be incorporated at different stages of the assessment process, and not necessarily as one concrete topic. It is however, advisable to allocate some time at the very end of the last assessment session to review and summarize the items presented below.

### *Education in the cognitive-behavioural model*

The client must have an understanding of the cognitive model in order to be able to move forward and make progress in treatment. To this end, it is essential that the client has a good understanding and grasp of the key components of the model, such as association and causal relationships between cognition, affect, behaviour, craving and using. This is best achieved using the client's own data, that is using the information obtained in the assessment from the developmental profile and functional analysis, to illustrate the cognitive model. In this way, the client starts to understand him/herself in the context of the model. Some clients will not have a psychological understanding of the nature of their problem, so it may be necessary to use some of the cognitive techniques described above. Using common examples of how thought processes work in different situations may be a useful way to start with, so that the client can understand how thoughts and behaviours interact.

***Example***
When learning to drive, you need to think carefully about all of the processes involved, for example starting the car and using the gearbox. With experience, these behaviours become automatic and you don't need to think about them. However, if you have to drive on the Continent, you may find that you have to think more carefully again, for example about which lane you are driving in and which way to turn.

It may be helpful to ask the client to think about some common examples of his own and work through them before moving on to drug-related situations. As already mentioned, this part of the assessment can take place at the very beginning if considered necessary. It is also important to highlight here that the therapist should use a language which is understood by the client, and avoid terminology if it is not clearly explained and understood.

### *Negotiation of treatment goals and rules of therapy*

Using the above information, a plan for the treatment is made between the therapist and the client. This means that the topics to be covered, the order and priority will be agreed. This may of course change in the course of the treatment. The therapist also needs to discuss with clients what they want to gain from the treatment. Some of this information will have already been obtained from the assessment, but it is important to summarize it so that both the therapist and client are clear about what they are aiming for in treatment. The therapist also explains to the client the 'rules' of therapy, that is the importance of attending sessions, doing out-of-session assignments, giving the therapist notice if the client cannot attend an appointment and rescheduling it, attending for urine tests and key worker appointments.

### *Getting ready to start therapy*

Now you have your case formulation ready, and you have discussed it with the client; so you are ready to progress to the first session. Before starting, you need to plan the therapy sessions with the client. This involves discussing the topics to be covered and the order in which they will be covered. This should not be set in stone, as reformulation, addition of extra sessions within a topic, or incorporating elective topics might be necessary. It is important to keep in mind throughout that clients need to achieve

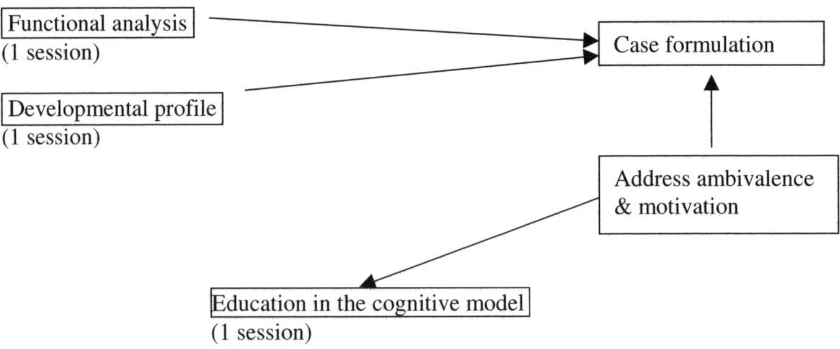


**Figure 5.4** Summary of assessment process.

a positive experience from therapy in order to enhance their engagement, promote compliance and increase self-confidence. The aim should be to address the most important aspects of the substance use problem, but to set easily achievable aims using graded task assignment at the beginning of the treatment in order to facilitate this. Clients can easily lose motivation by 'failing' early in therapy, because they are vulnerable. This reinforces core beliefs, so a success experience that is an assignment carried out with a successful outcome, can be used as evidence to challenge such beliefs (Figure 5.4).

CHAPTER SIX

# Core topics

## Core topic 1: Building and maintaining motivation for change

### *Introduction*

Motivational interviewing (MI) is an effective evidence-based approach for enhancing motivation to make desired changes in behaviour or lifestyle. Overcoming ambivalence about change is often the major barrier for many clients, even when the need to make that change has been recognized. The principles and techniques of MI can be effective in reducing risk behaviours such as substance misuse, smoking, unprotected sexual activity and harmful eating behaviours, as well as increasing compliance with diet/exercise in diabetes, hypertension or cardiac rehabilitation, or compliance with medication in patients with chronic psychiatric problems. This approach can also be used for facilitative information feedback to clients and to provide opportunistic interventions for service users in general settings who are not being seen specifically for treatment of risk behaviours.

The MI topic described here is about identifying and exploring ambivalence and enhancing motivation using two 'eliciting change talk' (Miller and Rollnick, 2002) techniques in addition to the core strategies of MI. The two techniques, using the decision-balance matrix and the importance and confidence rulers, are supplemented (or replaced, if the client is already at the action stage of motivation for change) with part of the session devoted to helping the client move himself into planning the next stages of treatment.

As described earlier, maintaining motivation to change behaviour (or stick with a change) is vital when doing any of the CBT topics described in this book. Ambivalence about attending the session may be present, there may be signs of resistance during the CBT topic or the client may simply not be at the motivational stage of change for CBT (i.e. they may still be contemplative or even pre-contemplative either about the need for attending the CBT session or about changing their alcohol/drug use). A person's motivation for change will fluctuate depending on many factors. Most people have a degree of ambivalence, a number of reasons for and against giving up or changing a habit, and the salience given to each of these can fluctuate even in a short time period. Thus, it may be necessary in any session to move away from the more directive CBT topic back to an MI style of working. The present topic can be used as a standalone or it can be reverted to within another topic if resistance or reluctance is encountered. As stated above, as a standalone topic it can be used to lead to further programme planning by including a plan of action, that is moving from the building motivation phase of MI to the action phase. An important point to remember when doing this session is that MI is not simply about techniques, it is about the approach and style adopted by the therapist (described earlier).

### Aims of the topic

This topic aims in part to introduce the concept of 'stages of change' to the client, but more importantly to address any ambivalence and shore up motivation. This is done by the client weighing up the advantages and disadvantages of changing/not changing and proposing reasons for change. It also facilitates the client's understanding of his own reasons for change and confidence to achieve it, as well as understanding better any barriers or difficulties he may have in maintaining resolve. If appropriate (i.e. if the client is in the action phase of MI), this session might progress to the development of a plan of action for implementing change and to help inform the need for other topics to be covered.

### Outline of the topic content and the techniques used

In this topic you will provide the rationale for the cognitive model if it has not already been done, and in particular the relevance of motivation to this. Give (hypothetical) examples of how motivation has been the crucial factor for others in maintaining abstinence from illicit drugs or in relapsing/not relapsing to excessive drinking. Personalize it to the client by asking him about the impact of his resolve to adhere to his intentions has on actual drinking and other such addictions (e.g. what impact does level of motivation have on substance use or lifestyle?).

***Using the motivational stages of change model*** In this part of the session you will be explaining the stages of change model of motivation for change. It might be useful to create a visual aid for the model and with prompts from you, get the client to describe examples of the different stages of change.

***Using the decision-balance matrix*** State that this topic includes a discussion of positive and negative effects of alcohol and drug use, both short and long term. If appropriate to the client, do this first of all for another activity, for example sport. Brainstorm with the decision-balance matrix on a flipchart or paper (possibly using the record sheet given in Appendix I).

Next, with open-ended questions but using predominantly reflective statements with frequent summaries, encourage the client to explore each of the stated benefits/negatives of using/not using. Try not to find yourself in the position of pressing the client to give the 'right' answers, and reflect both sides of the argument.

***Example***
'Tell me more about what you enjoy about drinking', 'Tell me more about the last time you argued with your partner about your drinking'. 'Not feeling ill is obviously a benefit of using; what part does using have in causing you to feel ill?'

***Using the importance and confidence rulers*** The ruler is an imaginary one and it consists of a rating scale that goes from 0 (not at all important/no confidence) to 10 (most important issue in my life at the moment/100 % confident, I can do this). Remember the two key questions:

'How important is it for you to drink less in the future?'

'How confident are you that if you did cut down, you could stick at it?'

Ask the client to rate each on a scale of 0–10. Further questions:

'Why a score of 6 and not 0?'
(i.e. the client gives you the reasons for change/saying what gives him some confidence)

'What would it take/what would have to happen for the score to move from 6 to 9?'
(i.e. the client states the further risks of continuing to drink or of not changing injecting behaviours/is saying what would boost confidence further).

For the importance ruler, remember not to ask 'why are you at a 6 and not 10?' (you are putting the client into the position of arguing/giving the reasons why it is not such an important problem).

***Developing a plan of action (if appropriate)*** This 'action phase' of MI has a number of components, each with a number of steps (see Miller and Rollnick, 2002, for details).

*Recapitulation* This is the first component and involves the following steps:

- A summary of the client's own perceptions of the problem, as reflected in his self-motivational statements.
- A summing-up of the client's ambivalence, including what remains positive or attractive about the problem behaviour.
- A review of whatever objective evidence you have regarding the presence of risks and problems.
- A restatement of any indications the client has offered of wanting, intending or planning to change.
- Your own assessment of the client's situation, particularly at points where it converges with the client's own concerns.

*Synthesis* This is based on Socratic questioning and is essentially asking 'What next?' Possible key questions might be:

What do you think you will do?

What does this mean about your drinking?

It must be uncomfortable for you now, seeing all this... What's the next step?

What do you think has to change?

What could you do? What are your options?

It sounds like things can't stay the way they are now. What are you going to do?

Of the things I have mentioned here, which for you are the most important reasons for a change? How are you going to do it?

What's going to happen now? Where do we go from here?

How would you like things to turn out for you now, ideally?

What concerns you about changing your drinking?

What would be some of the good things about stopping injecting?

*Advice* It may be appropriate for the therapist to offer information and advice, but always in the style of MI!

- Play hard to get–only give advice when pressed or invited to do so by the client. You might ask, 'would it be OK if I gave you some of my thoughts on this?' Or 'I don't know if this would work for you, but other people with these kinds of problems have been helped by. . . '
- Qualify any suggestions ('this is helpful for some people but not everyone'; 'other people drinking roughly similar amounts seem to benefit most from. . . ')
- Offer several options, the client chooses.

*Negotiation* Negotiate a plan with the client. This will involve:

- Setting goals

  What is it you want to change?
  What are the consequences of change (what might go wrong)?

- Considering change options: This will involve: (i) a 'menu' approach, with several options available; (ii) advice on 'matching' appropriate options with action and desired outcome; and (iii) encouragement not to be discouraged by 'failure'.

***Arriving at a plan*** Create a change plan worksheet including desirable changes, reasons for wanting the changes, necessary steps to achieve them, ways that other people can help, indications of success and potential problems (Miller & Rollnick, 2002). If possible, get the client to do the writing and ask where he will be able to keep it as a record of what he wants to do. If it is not appropriate to use the worksheet (e.g. if the client has reading/writing difficulties or for some reason is unwilling to use a written record), just use the headings for discussion.

Finally, check out the client's commitment to the plan (ask if this is what they are confident they want to do) and ensure with the client and any other services that this transition to the action stage of treatment can go ahead (e.g. there is not a lengthy waiting list for prescribing, etc.).

***Out-of-session practise for this topic***

Ask the client what they might practise from this topic that might be helpful in keeping their motivation up. Give an example such as:

- Make a list of the main reasons for sticking with the programme and/or reducing drug/alcohol use. Ask whether or not it might be useful to keep the list handy for times when their resolve is low or when they are aware of being at risk of drinking/using more than intended. Or:
- For each of the advantages and disadvantages write down a 'weighting' from 0 to 10 how important to you each is. What's the total for each list? Read through this at least once each day. (Revert to full MI if the total score for advantages outweighs that for disadvantages!) Or:
- Ask the client to decide on three times each day when he could be prompted by something (anything that regularly happens that's not alcohol/drug related such as having a non-alcoholic drink, travelling or other activity) into asking themselves the importance and confidence ruler questions. Have these questions written down and emphasize to the client to take time to think through their answer. Or:
- If appropriate, discuss with a non-drinker/drug user you know is likely to be supportive of your efforts to change, what your advantages and disadvantages of change/not changing are. Or:
- Choose an action point from the change plan worksheet, get the client to break this into steps for them to do between sessions.

Remember either to role-play with the client what they are going to practise, or in some way go through in detail with them an example of their out-of-session practise. Questions such as, 'Tell me when you could do this and what might get in the way', are useful.

## ► Core topic 2: Identifying and dealing with stimulus conditions (the client's high-risk situations, emotions or thoughts) and developing an all-purpose coping plan

### *Introduction*

Stimulus conditions or high-risk situations can broadly be defined as situations in which the client encounters substance-related antecedents, triggers or cues for being at risk of lapsing. Their nature may vary considerably, but they can broadly be described as internal (beliefs and/or emotional states) and external (situations, cues). Following a brief overview of the rationale for CBT-based prevention of relapse (but personalized to each individual case), the therapist and the client should work together to develop a list of the more problematic stimulus conditions. This can be done either from memory of examples over the past few weeks, discussion of previous lapses or using hypothetical case scenarios of what could lead up to a lapse for the client. The stimulus may be difficult for the client to identify because of the interactive nature of emotional states and external events, or it may be so pervasive that the client is not able to see the process clearly. This is where the functional analysis is very important, and it may be necessary to use a number of the techniques described to enable the client and therapist to understand the process. The process may or may not involve craving. It is important to identify this and if craving is part of any stimulus condition, ensure Topic 3 (Coping with craving) is also covered (either before or after this one).

For some people in the maintenance stage of change, new stimulus conditions resulting from unforeseen circumstances may have to be faced. Anticipating as yet unknown stimulus conditions can be thought of as having a well-rehearsed fire drill; you can't say what will cause a future fire but knowing what to do is a worthwhile exercise, although as with a fire drill, you hope it will never need to be used 'for real'. Part of this topic covers an all-purpose coping plan for any unpredicted stimulus conditions.

### *Aims of the topic*

- To define what stimulus conditions are
- To identify the client's hierarchy of stimulus conditions
- To review what past and current coping strategies there are
- To anticipate future stimulus conditions
- To identify potential unpredictable events that could act as stimulus conditions for relapse
- To develop a personal generic coping plan.

### *Outline of the topic content and the techniques used*

***What are the stimulus conditions/high-risk situations?*** This part of the session includes a discussion of the typical high-risk situations for the client (again, from memory or diary of the last few weeks, recounting previous lapses or speculating what might lead up to a lapse). Explain to the client that 'a high-risk situation is any situation or condition that poses a threat to your sense of control and increases the risk of potential relapse'. Typical high-risk situations might be:

- physically being in a situation associated with drinking/using
- an emotional state such as feeling anxious, depressed, angry, frustrated, bored
- or perhaps the opposite, feeling good, wanting to celebrate a positive event
- interpersonal conflict (arguing with a friend, conflicts at home)
- social pressure to join in (i.e. others encouraging client to join them at the pub).

***Example***

'I had been doing really well for two weeks and had so much more time on my hands. Besides college I had no other plans since up to this all my free time was spent drinking. Come Saturday night I was bored and angry that I was making all this effort and getting nowhere fast. Without thinking, I found myself in one of my usual haunts, and got plastered as fast as I could'.

***What to do about stimulus conditions/high-risk situations*** The next step is to enable the client to explore how to cope with the high-risk situations and stimulus conditions. It is essential to review the client's existing coping strategies and the meaning they have for the client; this can be taken from the functional analysis. Developing adaptive strategies may involve:

**i.** Learning how to avoid the stimulus condition altogether, for example taking a different route home to avoid passing the dealer's house.

**ii.** Learning how to cope by confronting the stimulus situation and resist using by:

- challenging thoughts/beliefs–use the client's core and/or alcohol/drug beliefs from the case formulation or identified using cognitive techniques. Enable the client to challenge them by discussing thoughts and beliefs with a non-using friend or using self-dialogue. Flashcards may be useful reminders for clients outside therapy
- education about the process of craving/urges (see also Topic 3): 'They are common and normal and not a sign of failure. They are like ocean waves that become stronger, but only to a point, then they start to fade away. Without drug use, the urges will weaken and eventually go away'
- developing a specific behavioural plan for when a situation arises, for example going to a party that cannot be avoided, make specific arrangements about how to resist using for the duration.

It is important to emphasize that the ultimate aim is to enable the client to cope with stimulus situations as avoidance is not always possible. In the earlier stages of treatment avoidance may be the best option until the client has built up a repertoire of coping skills and other 'core topics' have been addressed.

***Specific examples of stimulus conditions*** Here we present in more detail some possible/common stimulus conditions and suggestions of how to address them during the session. Remember that these are only suggestions, which follow the points outlined above and the aim is to enable the client to develop their own coping plan.

**Rows** Interpersonal conflicts are situations involving an ongoing or relatively recent conflict associated with any interpersonal (one-to-one) relationship such as a parent, friendship, family members or people at school/college.

***Example***

'I went to see a social worker who was arranging a move from a hostel to a flat for me. I had to wait about twenty minutes, then I discovered that my application was still being processed after one month. Well, I blew my top, told everyone where to get off, and got into an argument with the head of the social services department. I left feeling helpless and that I was at the mercy of the system. The only way to get rid of this headache was to use, so I went out and bought some gear'.

*How to cope*

- Get out of the situation
- In future plan ahead, think about the different possible things that could go well/not well and plan how to react
- Learn to be assertive instead of aggressive (see Chapter 7)

**Joining the club** These are situations where a person is responding to the influence of another person or group of people who exert pressure to engage in the addictive behaviour (see Core topic 4).

***Example***

'My dealer had been phoning me. So far I had been putting her off, because I had started the treatment programme. The thing is, she wasn't happy about losing such a valuable customer so she came round to my place. I felt pressured and bought two days supply of heroin.'

*How to cope*

- Avoid
- Plan ahead
- Find excuses
- Get help from friends
- Practise what to say/ways of being assertive.

**Coping with a lapse** Discuss and later on role-play with the client the main steps involved.

- Stop, look and listen
  When a lapse occurs stop what you are doing and think. This is a warning that you are in danger. Think of it like a flat tyre: the driver stops at a safe place to sort it out.
- Keep calm
  Remember, one slip does not make a total relapse. A slip does not mean you are a failure and have no will power or that you are a hopeless addict. There is no failure only feedback. It is an opportunity to learn. Let the feeling of 'I have started so I might as well finish' pass. Avoid the idea 'Well, I might as well go for a total

bender'. The more you can learn from a lapse, the less likely it will lead to a total relapse.

- Review your commitment
  Recall your decision to kick the habit. Weigh up the short- and long-term benefits of abstinence. Remember how far you have come in the journey of habit change. Do you really believe that a single slip cancels out all the progress you have made up to now? Renew your motivation and commitment.
- Review the situation leading up to the lapse
  What events led up to the slip? Were there any early-warning signals that you missed? What was the high-risk situation? You may get new information concerning the sources of stress in your life. There may be thoughts and feelings that the effects of the drug taken during the slip are going to overpower you and make it impossible for you to regain control.
- Make an *immediate* plan of action for recovery
  Get rid of all drugs/alcohol.
  Remove yourself from the high-risk situation. Take a walk. Leave the scene.
- Ask for help
  Make it easy for yourself. Ask friends or relatives. Telephone the drugs helpline.

**Coping with anger** *How to do it*

- Express it in words rather than actions
- Get rid of the feelings through exercise
- Hit something safe, like a punch-bag
- Distract yourself
- Go shopping. Buy something
- Why not go to the cinema/theatre/park. . . ? Watch a video.

***Coping with craving (see also next core topic)*** *How to do it*

- Recognize the craving
- Use a brief relaxation technique
- Make positive self-statements
- Distract yourself from the thoughts and feelings
- Go with the craving
- Recall negative consequences
- Use a craving diary.

Use the above to help form a hierarchy of risks and to inform future sessions.

*Anticipating unpredictable future stimulus conditions* Life is unpredictable and not all specific stimulus conditions can be anticipated. Generalizations of the kinds of events that could become problematic are, however, possible. Crises, negative life events (learning that one is HIV positive, loss of an important relationship), and even positive events (receiving a large amount of money, starting a new relationship) can become a stimulus condition. Even without knowing the specifics, it is still possible to develop the equivalent of a 'fire drill'.

*Developing a personal generic coping plan* When clients are stressed, they are more likely to use old coping strategies rather than healthier new ones. It is therefore important for the client to try to develop a generic coping strategy that can be adapted to any major crises. This could include:

- A set of important phone numbers of supportive others who can be relied upon
- Recall of negative consequences of returning to use
- A set of positive thoughts which can be substituted for drink or drug-related thoughts
- A set of reliable distracters
- A list of safe places where the client can ride out the crises with few cues or temptations to use, for example parents or non-drug using friend's house.

Flashcards may be useful for some of these strategies.

### *Out-of-session practise for this topic*

Ask the client what they might practise from this session that might be helpful in avoiding or coping with high-risk situations. Give an example such as:

- Keep a daily diary (see example in Appendix IV) of your risky situations, moods or thoughts. Identify how you coped.
- Practise one of the skills identified above as ways of coping. If appropriate (e.g. going into the supermarket to buy cigarettes and avoid the wine shelves) arrange for this to be done in a gradual way so that success can be guaranteed at each step.
- Think about a risky situation coming up before the next session. With the therapist in this session, write a plan of what you are going to do to avoid or cope with it. Practise this before the situation if possible, and write in your diary how this coping plan worked out.
- Make a list of your own coping plans, people to contact, things to do, places you can go to and other things if an unpredicted crisis or event occurs.

Remember either to role-play with the client what they are going to practise, or in some way go through in detail with them an example of their out-of-session practise.

'Tell me when you could do this and what might get in the way of doing this' are useful questions.



## Core topic 3: Coping with craving

### *Introduction*

Craving can be thought of as the subjective desire to experience the effects or consequences of alcohol/drug taking. The feeling of craving is not experienced by all clients. Craving can, however, be intense and for some it is the major reason for lapsing back to drinking, using illicit drugs, among others. Cravings vary in intensity and frequency: they may range from a fleeting feeling to pacing around for hours totally dominated by feelings and thoughts about the substance or behaviour. They also vary in the way they are experienced by different people. It is important to identify whether craving is experienced by the client and whether it is part of any stimulus condition (see core topic 2) likely to trigger a risk of lapse. It is important for the client to recognize that cravings are common and normal, and can occur sometimes even after several years of abstinence. The experience and nature of craving can be assessed through self-report:

Can you describe what it feels like for you to be craving?

How bothered are you by craving?

### *Aims of the topic*

- To realize what we understand by 'craving'
- To identify the person's own experience of craving and what it involves
- To identify craving triggers that may be different for different individuals
- To increase awareness of situations which lead to craving
- To identify appropriate ways of coping with craving.

### *Outline of the topic content and the techniques used*

First of all it is useful to know what, if any, skills the client already has for coping with craving. Simply asking, 'What do you need to do to counter these experiences of craving?', may answer what skills the client is already using. If the client already has suggestions, then do not force others on them, but focus on an exercise that builds on or reinforces their way. On the other hand, the following is a suggested course of action that has been shown to help some people be prepared to cope with craving. After outlining the following steps of action ask the client, 'What do you feel would work best for you?' This subtopic can then be discussed in further detail, possibly over several sessions.

***Recognize the craving and its triggers*** First and foremost you need to recognize that you are craving. This sounds obvious but the feeling may creep up on you. It is important to stand back and observe yourself. If you are not very aware of your moods and feelings then it might be important to start working toward becoming more aware of them. That means trying to find out what triggers your cravings.

This is the first step to alerting you to either avoid them or prepare for them. As well as certain moods and feelings, many people have become aware that exposure to cues associated with their addictive behaviour can give rise to cravings. Such cues could involve drug paraphernalia (e.g. needles or spoons), smells (e.g. of alcohol), places and/or people associated with drinking, using drugs and so on.

Once you are able to say to yourself 'I'm craving' you are in a position to do something about it. Look for craving triggers.

Remember, for some clients, especially early in treatment, avoidance of triggers is the most viable way of coping. Avoidance may be straightforward: not going to your dealer, not using other drugs, not going to the pub and so on. On the other hand it may be impossible (spoons are part of everyday life), or it may involve major lifestyle changes or breaking ties. Some clients are able to gain better insight into their cravings by keeping a craving diary, which should include date, time, description of the situation, emotional state when started, strength and duration (Carroll, 1998). This involves recording every time that they experience a craving. If the client feels as if they are always craving, it is better to start with the times when the craving gets worse. Please make sure that you have fully explained to the client how to keep the diary. Modify the format of the diary to make it friendly and easy for use by the client.

***Use of brief relaxation techniques*** The first thing to do is to take a bit of space and calm down. Do you have your own individual way of relaxing? If not, you may find it useful and helpful to learn a brief relaxation technique that only takes a few seconds or minutes to perform. One such technique is controlled breathing and another is progressive relaxation. The first is a breathing exercise and the second consists of gradually tensing and relaxing the various muscle groups in your body. Which way do you prefer?

***Positive self-statements*** You may need to say something to yourself which challenges the good thoughts about drugs and/or alcohol (also, the decisional balance matrix about short- and long-term positive and negative consequences in the previous session might be helpful for drawing your attention to the negative effects of using.) The things that you say to yourself should not be too complicated, and they should remind you of the positive things that you are getting by not using.

It might be helpful to remember the following:

- Self-statements which involve the thought of stopping for someone else usually don't work very well. It is better to make statements about stopping that involve something you want for yourself.

- Try to avoid self-statements that have a punishing side to them, like 'If I don't do it then I'm...'
- Try to avoid shock-horror statements, or balance these with positive outcomes. That is, memories of awful things that have happened are better balanced with notions of feeling healthier, for example.
- Try to say something to yourself which you really believe.
- Some people find using phrases and statements false and unconvincing. In this case it might be better to use images of scenes or memories that are pleasant and relevant to you.

What can you think of to say to yourself that will help you?

***Distraction*** After this, you may need to find something to do to use up some of your frustrated energy and to distract you from concentrating on the craving experience. Whatever you choose to do, it needs to be something that is very absorbing mentally and takes all of your concentration. Many people find that physical activities are particularly useful for this. The activity should also be interesting and enjoyable. It seems to help if the activity lasts for a reasonable period of time (e.g. half an hour or more).

Can you think of any activity that has any of these qualities for you?

Can you think of any activities that you may have used in the past to distract yourself from something?

Can you identify which of these you felt have worked and which haven't?

***Going with the craving*** The idea here is to let cravings occur, peak and pass. 'You experience the craving without either fighting or giving into them.' Encourage your client to use imagery, for example walking over a hill (it's a struggle going up but eventually it's an easy downhill), surfing the craving feeling or seeing examples of when the client has successfully overcome a difficult task (possibly a previous example of riding out cravings). Judo analogy (as in handling resistance) can also be used ('you use your opponent's momentum to your advantage rather than fighting it direct'). Another image might be thinking of craving as 'like ocean waves that get stronger but only to a point, then they start to fade away. Without drug use, the urges will weaken and eventually go away. The purpose is not to make the cravings disappear, but by riding them out you are learning to experience them as less unpleasant, and as not having the inevitable consequence of having to have a drink, inject or use on top, etc'.

***Recalling negative consequences*** Positive outcome expectancies often occur and the negative consequences are forgotten. Revisit the lists made up in Topic 1 of positives and negatives of using. Ask the client to keep it handy (as in that topic).

### *Out-of-session practise for this topic*

Ask the client what they might practise from this topic that might be helpful in coping with craving. Give an example such as:

Keep a daily craving diary. Add a column for how you coped.

Practice one of the subtopic skills identified above as ways of coping.

If practising relaxation exercises, do these at least once a day, starting at times when you feel already reasonably relaxed. Once mastered, try to practise at times of craving.

For positive and negative images or thoughts about using/not using, write these down on a card if possible. Keep this card for use when you are craving (see Appendix I).

For distraction, make sure it's a positive distraction (something you enjoy).

Remember either to role-play with the client what they are going to practise, or in some way go through in detail an example of their out-of-session practise. 'Tell me when you could do this and what might get in the way of doing this' are useful questions.

## ▶ Core topic 4: Refusal skills, handling confrontations and building assertiveness

### *Introduction*

A major issue for many alcohol or drug users is having and using skills of assertiveness. Examples include being able to handle awkward social situations such as complaining to someone or even just asking for directions, dealing with confrontations, saying no to reasonable requests without feeling guilty, saying no to unreasonable requests without getting angry and so on. For some drinkers/drug users, refusing offers that will lead to drinking and other such addictions (well-intentioned and accidental or not) can be a major problem and lead to a high-risk situation for using. Refusing may be difficult because the lifestyle of many substance users may be orientated around other users including drug dealers or habitual drinkers. The social network of some drinkers and drug users may involve predominantly other drinkers/drug users, so social isolation may become an issue in attempting to reduce contact with this network. Many clients lack the basic skills (or are easily persuaded not to use their skills) to refuse offers of indulgence. For others, refusing a drink may not be the problem, the problem is the stress and consequent low self-esteem created by being unassertive in relationships, at work or at home, leading to feelings of being put-on, used by others or the feeling of not being in control of events which may lead to drinking or using as a way of coping. This topic covers a number of areas but focuses on handling the social network (i.e. the people, associates/acquaintances, community structures) which support continued drinking/drug use.

### *Aims of the topic*

- To increase the client's awareness of assertion, and how to use it
- Assessment of the client's network support for drinking/drug use availability and of the steps needed to change this support or availability
- Exploration of strategies for breaking contact with individuals who facilitate continued drinking or who supply drugs
- To introduce techniques of assertion including learning and practising refusal skills and handling confrontations.

### *Outline of the topic content and the techniques used*

***Discussion of what is meant by being 'Assertive'*** Assertiveness is a method of attaining rights without denying the rights of others. The following are the characteristics of assertive people:

- feel free of fear
- let go of restricting beliefs
- are prepared to take a risk
- know they can make a choice
- express feelings openly
- know what they want
- give and take compliments easily
- give and take fair criticism.

Outline with the client the following four types of behaviour and get them to consider which type they commonly use and in what situations:

*Aggressive* Becoming aggravated and over-reacting to a situation. Often this is due to a build up of passive behaviour. Aggressive people react in an inappropriate manner to a situation, usually with physical or verbal violence; they violate other people's rights through aggression or manipulation.

Feelings and results:

Feelings of power and satisfaction; relief at expressing pent-up feelings; shame and disappointment; embarrassment; domination of passive people; intolerance of defeat; success through power.

*Passive* Letting or even forcing people to make decisions for oneself; ignoring one's own feelings and keeping opinions private.

Feelings and results:

Avoid friction and conflict; martyrdom and generosity; frustration and helplessness; disappointment; resentment of oneself and others; build up of resentment released through explosion; physical and mental stress; inability to make decisions or express opinions. May be known as easy to get along with...or spineless, a bit of a doormat!

*Indirect* Expressing wants through roundabout actions, words, behaviours. Pretending and making excuses in order to get what one wants.

Feelings and results:

Power and success; dishonesty and sneakiness; chance of being misunderstood; relationships built on deceit and manipulation; reputation of insincerity and deception; helplessness and frustration.

*Assertive* Saying what one means in an honest, direct and appropriate manner and doing so without violating someone else's rights. Being able to express one's own feelings, both positive and negative, without having to apologize.

Feelings and results:

Self-respect and confidence; honesty in relationships with others (people know where they stand, that you are being truthful); feelings of doubt about one's right to assert oneself; some conflict between you and others, especially if they are not comfortable with assertiveness; independence/feeling of autonomy and self-efficacy.

***Assessment of client's network support for drinking/drug use availability and of the steps needed to change this support or availability*** Discuss with the client who they drink with, the circumstances surrounding their drinking:

- Who are the client's social network support for drinking/using?
- Is the client involved in selling drugs?
- Does the client live with/or work with other drinkers?
- What steps if any has the client already taken towards reducing availability?
- Has the client informed other drinkers/drug-using friends of their intention to stop using?
- Has the client attempted to remove himself from the distribution network?

***Exploration of strategies for breaking contact with individuals who facilitate continued drinking or who supply drugs*** What kind of relationship does the client have with such individuals? What needs to happen for the client to avoid or handle such people or circumstances, either in terms of changing the environment supporting drinking or dealing with the people concerned assertively? If the relationship is intimate then breaking contact completely may be difficult; in such a case negotiation and development of alternative strategies may be necessary, for example asking partner not to drink alcohol or use heroin at home, or asking partner not to insist on being in what for the client are very high-risk situations.

***Assessment of client's network support for not misusing substance*** What help and support can the client mobilize from non-drinkers in their network? What needs to happen to make their support more available/likely to happen?

**

***Techniques of assertion (Learning and practising refusal skills and handling confrontations)*** *Saying no to Unreasonable Requests* An unreasonable request is one you know most other people would say no to, or one where you feel you want to say no but instead find yourself saying yes, or one you later regret or have to lie/escape from in a way that lowers your self-esteem or impacts negatively on your relationship with the person!

A good, assertive response to an unreasonable request involves:

- Acknowledging the request and the reasons the person is making it
- Maintaining good eye contact and a relaxed, confident posture
- Giving a clear firm 'no' without offering an apology; it is an unreasonable request after all, so saying 'No, I'm sorry but I can't do that for you' makes it sound as if you're at fault
- No excuses: giving an excuse, even if it is true, leaves the door open to ways round the excuse ('I can't lend you any money because I need to pay the electricity' could leave you open to 'But if you just pay part of the bill they'll accept that!').

Role-play with the client: the following answer is the only one allowed (this makes it easier and more fun)–'I can see your problem but no, I can't. . . '

Examples of unreasonable requests, to be followed with examples the client can think of that are more realistic to their lives:

'I'm going away for a few weeks, would you mind having my cannabis plants and watering them for me?' ('I can see your problem, but no, I can't do that for you'.)

'I've got no money for the washing machine, can you put my washing in with yours!'

'Can you give me a lift to the airport next Friday night at 2 a.m?'

'I don't want to risk parking my new car in the town centre, can I borrow yours to go shopping?'

'Can you lend me a thousand pounds/that expensive new dress you have for a party?'

Make up your own unreasonable requests, they should be extreme, amusing and unrealistic so that the client can easily say no. Once this is mastered, using the reply above, get the more realistic examples from the client. To begin with, reverse the role-play so that the client is asking you and your task is to model an assertive response following the guidelines above.

*Handling confrontation assertively – the DESC routine* Remember, the aim of assertive confrontation is to solve a problem with another person while maintaining the self-respect of both. The DESC routine provides a way of remembering how to solve a problem assertively. It stands for describe, express, specify and consequences.

- Describe
  Make a factual, non-blaming statement of what has happened. For example, 'In the office just now you told me off in front of two other people'.
- Express
  Say how you felt. For example, 'I was embarrassed and annoyed'.
- Specify
  Say exactly what you would like the other to do. For example, 'In future, if you want to criticize me, please wait until we are on our own'.
- Consequences
  Say what will happen if you both agree. For example, 'If you do, I'll be able to pay attention and learn, and we'll get on better'.

The process is one of negotiation. This means: (i) when appropriate, be prepared to back down and find a compromise which satisfies the needs of both people (however, keep your goal clearly in mind and don't get side tracked onto other issues); (ii) make sure that you both know exactly what has been agreed; (iiii) express appreciation of the other person's agreement to change, and your own eagerness to keep the bargain; (iv) stop. Don't go on and on trying to resolve more and more issues.

Role-play an easy example to begin with, and swap roles with the client. For example, role-play taking a faulty kettle back to a shop.

You don't want a replacement (you've lost confidence in the shop), you don't want a voucher, you're not willing to return when the manager is available and so on. You're not prepared to accept you may have damaged the kettle at home (you didn't). You want a cash refund. Use DESC with the above techniques to get what you want without being aggressive or threatening (the consequence of getting what you want could be that you are more likely to shop there in the future).

Move onto a real-life example 'closer to home'. This needs planning beforehand with the client and you should model DESC before getting the client to try it.

### *Additional techniques*

- Broken record
  Repeat your main point in the same calm tone (i.e. the needle on the vinyl record has got stuck, you can rephrase the message even though the meaning is the same!).
- Disagree; say simply, 'I don't agree'.
- Emphasize feelings.
  Repeat your statement of how you felt, saying this is important to you.
- Agree... But...
  Admit the other person's point of view but repeat that yours is different.
- Dismiss detours
  Ignore side-tracks onto other issues, or say that they are not relevant.

- Redefine
  Don't accept the other person's negative label. Restate your positive opinion of how you have acted.
- Question
  Don't accept vague criticism. Ask for clarification (e.g. 'In what ways did you think I was being stupid?')

## State negative consequences

If there is no alternative, promise realistic negative consequences if the other does not change. However, this can lead to escalating anger. Also, making unrealistic threats (which cannot be carried out) provokes more negative behaviour.

### *Out-of-session practise for this topic*

Ask the client what they might practise from this topic that might be helpful for assertiveness, handling confrontations, refusal skills. Ensure that the client is not setting himself up for a situation he can't handle, things getting out of hand, arguments with someone he is unlikely to win/defeat and other similar situations. Stress that as with most changes, they're best done gradually and in small steps. Give an example that could be a first step such as:

- Make one reasonable request per day, that is asking for tap water with your meal in a café, asking directions, asking for something to be passed to you. Get the client to record the situations, how they felt and what happened as a consequence of asking.
- Pay a (genuine) compliment to someone they know (perhaps a different person each day). Again, record this as above.
- Next steps might be the client practising saying 'no' to requests where she wants to say 'no' and involve people with whom she is not in personal relationship with. Then move on to more personal relationships.
- From the items identified in looking at the social networks supporting drinking/drugs and those supporting not drinking/drugs, choose with the client a step-by-step approach to changing the former and facilitating the latter. With the client, compile an action plan they sign up to and can work on outside the session. This could even (with the client's consent) involve the therapist contacting those who the client identifies as supportive of not using/drinking. It is preferable and consistent with enhancing autonomy and assertiveness if the client does this themselves, but if they are so unassertive as to mean this would be very unlikely to happen, then you contact them!

For the plan of action for changing the social network contacts supporting continued drinking/drug use, make sure a vacuum is not created or social reinforcements are not being removed without the possibility of replacement reinforcements. With all of the above, role-play and practise in the session how the client will practise outside the session.

## Core topic 5: Wise decision taking at choice points

### *Introduction*

Seemingly irrelevant decisions (SIDs) refer to those decisions, rationalizations and minimizations of risk that move clients closer to or even into high-risk situations, although they seem unrelated to drinking/drug use. It is the classic 'one thing led to another' situation, a chain of events which by themselves seem unrelated to ending up in a high-risk situation. These are sometimes known as 'set ups'. For the drinker or drug user they can lead to lapses and relapse if the individual is not able to recognize and cope with them at an early stage. Each stage can be seen as giving an opportunity for a choice to be made that takes the person along a different route, leading away from lapsing.

This topic is a supplement to previous ones in which the client has learned how to identify, anticipate and cope with stimulus situations, cravings, and so on. Some of these situations may not be anticipated, some may be internal and impossible to avoid. For such situations this topic will help the client to identify the role of decisions made early in the chain that lead to vulnerability. Some clients may not be aware of how they ended up using drugs in some situations ('I didn't plan to have a drink, it just happened').

#### *Examples of relapse scenarios involving chains of events and potential choice points*

*Peter's Shopping* Peter is a car body repair/spray paint specialist. Business was very good and his boss was always trying to get him to do overtime. Today, Friday, he knew he had to leave work on time to get something to eat before meeting up with his friends to play snooker at the local pub. He had planned to stick to two pints only and stay away from any offers of drugs or going on to party into the night. As his boss was more pressing than ever to finish a car, he ended up staying until 7 p.m.. He tried to get out during the day to get his money for the weekend and weekend shopping but this proved impossible. As a consequence, he had to go after work which meant risking going past his old pub when it would be busy and all of his ex-drinking friends would be there as they always were on a Friday at that time. It also meant having to double back to the local shop where he had planned to buy his food for his evening meal.

Peter passed his old pub without seeing anyone he knew and got his money for the weekend. He was feeling tired and stressed and the thought of walking back to the shop just felt too much for him. He remembered his old pub did food and he thought that he was fine now for going in there, after all he had done really well in the last few months, with full control over his drinking and no drugs whatsoever. He thought that if he had one drink with a meal he could get home in time to get changed and ready for the snooker night out. Unfortunately once inside the pub and with so many people welcoming him and asking to buy him a beer... Well, he never made it to the snooker or even get some food, and after the fourth pint, the cocaine on offer was just too tempting.

*Susie's Dilemma* Susie had been in and out of rehabs a few times and had relapsed back into heroin and cocaine each time. This time she was determined not to pretend she could abstain completely and instead accept that the methadone programme was her best option, at least for the next year. She has three teenage children all living with her mother and an eight-year-old daughter in care. Susie had managed to cope with the child with the help of her husband but they had recently split up. Her husband (second marriage) had tried to look after the girl but couldn't because of his own drink and drug problem and money problems. When Susie suffered a big relapse her mother made it clear she was now too old to look after another granddaughter and the social worker felt there was no other option for the girl. Susie felt devastated over her marriage and her children, and wanted to show everyone that she could be a good mother and hold down a relationship without getting intoxicated all the time. She felt her methadone programme was her last hope.

Susie still had the tenancy on her two-bedroom flat but her income support was barely enough to live on. She decided to get a job (she used to work as a technician at the local hospital) and surprised herself with getting a job doing shift work in a local home for older people as a care assistant. The money was not great and the hours were very long, but it did give her extra money. She devised a plan of how she would be able to do up her flat, win back her teenage children's respect and possibly regain custody of the eight year old. It wasn't easy cleaning the flat, redecorating all of the rooms, and attempting to buy new furniture. But the worst problem was coping with taking methadone in the morning before work and knowing that was it for the rest of the day. Life started to become all work and no play. The pressure of long hours and trying to decorate became too much and she longed just to 'get out of it, just the once'. Then one of her teenage daughters asked to live with her and promptly announced she was pregnant once she had moved in. To cap it all, her ex-husband had started to visit her and came round smelling of alcohol. Susie was not coping with the stress in her life and yearned to be able to escape, but knew that if she did she would be giving up her last chance to prove herself. But then again she knew that her ex might this time be a better help to her and they could take it in turns to use, couldn't they?

### *Aims of the topic*

- To understand SIDs and their relationships to high-risk situations and lapses
- To identify personal examples of SIDs (potential or previously experienced)
- To rehearse and practise safe decision making and effective strategies when encountering such situations.

### *Outline of the topic content and the techniques used*

***Discuss the background to SIDs*** Often people make decisions which appear on the surface to be separate from the problem of self-control. These decisions, however, become a chain of events, which lead to a high-risk situation or such stress that it's 'not surprising' that they gave in. Often people then feel vindicated that they were not really responsible for the relapse or slip, thus eliciting sympathy rather than taking responsibility for their actions. Every person with an addiction must be aware of some of the set ups that they have used in the past. 'List some of the tricks of this kind that you have played on yourself in the past'. (You might prompt with a few examples from other people such as, getting into a row at home which always ends with me slamming the door saying 'I'm off to the pub, it's no surprise I need a drink', 'If you had my job with the long hours I do, you'd drink like me'.)

SIDs are dealt with firstly by recognizing them and the thoughts (and possibly feelings) that go with them; secondly by avoiding risky decision making and learning how to make choices that lead away from the 'road to a lapse'; and thirdly by developing coping skills for managing high-risk situations.

***Exercise for recognition of SIDs*** Read (or paraphrase) one (or both) of the stories above, which are about people making several SIDs that led to a high-risk situation and eventually relapse. Ask the client to pick out the decisions that were made along the way that led to situations where even a saint would not have been able to stick to their original intention. Acting earlier in the chain makes coping or avoidance possible. Ask at the choice points 'What do you think he/she was thinking, what were the statements/rationalization/excuse?'

***Developing the client's own relapse story*** Ask the client if they can think of their own relapse story. This should be based on a past experience or on what the client might imagine could get them into a 'set up'. Memories of a past relapse can be evoked simply by asking the client details of the last time this happened, and asking for elaboration about what led to each part of the 'set up'. If this is too difficult, a hypothetical 'set up' can be provoked, perhaps using imagery (although taking time to ensure the client is fully debriefed before leaving the session!).

Ask the client – 'Can you think of your own relapse story/Can you think of your own examples of where you have talked yourself or got yourself into a relapse situation? What were you telling yourself and how could you have interrupted the chain before the point of no return?'

Break the story into steps. It is important to identify what thoughts the client was experiencing and how they influenced the decisions made.

***Practise safe decision making*** Discuss with the client the possibility that if they can get into the habit of recognizing the small decisions made in the day, they can think through safe versus risky consequences for those decisions. This will make them less vulnerable to high-risk situations. It may also be helpful to ask about situations when the client coped successfully and identify the coping strategies used.

- Go back to the decision points in the story. Try to enable the client to detect the decisions that commonly occur at the beginning of the chain. What would have been safer decisions?

- Go through recent examples of safe versus risky decisions made by the client in real life.
- Give the following information on a handout to the client and discuss each SID with them.

*Common (Late in the chain) SIDs*

- Using other drugs such as alcohol, cocaine, cannabis and even some rituals associated with tobacco smoking. These can be triggers to wanting your favourite drug or may act to reduce your best intentions.
- Keeping alcohol and other such drugs in the house.
- Not destroying injecting or other illicit drug-associated paraphernalia.
- Going to pubs, parties or clubs where alcohol and other drugs are available.
- Mixing with drinkers, dealers and drug users who do not have your interests at heart.
- Keeping your problem a secret from people who do have your interests at heart.
- Not telling your drug-using associates of your decision to stick with your treatment programme.
- Not planning to fill free time.
- Having lots of unscheduled time at nights or weekends that can lead to boredom.
- Getting overtired, stressed, not eating a balanced diet.

'What can you add to this list from your knowledge of yourself or others?'

***Rational decision taking*** Ask the client to consider when making any decision, whether large or small, to do the following:

- Consider all the options
- Think about all the consequences, both positive and negative, for each of these options
- Select one of the options. Pick a safe decision that minimizes your risk of relapse
- Watch for 'red flag' thinking – thoughts like 'I have to...' or 'I can handle...' or 'it really doesn't matter if...' or 'I deserve a good night out...'

### *Out-of-session practise for this topic*

Ask the client to self-monitor decisions over the course of several days and, for each one, identify safer versus riskier decisions. The chart included in Appendix II might be useful.

## Core topic 6: Problem solving

### *Introduction*

Dealing with problems is something that we all have to do throughout our lives. However, sometimes the problems that we face seem overwhelming and beyond solving. For clients with severe substance misuse problems this is sometimes made worse because they have over time narrowed their repertoire to using drugs, or not developed a range of effective coping mechanisms for dealing with everyday problems that most people deal with as a matter of course. In addition to this, the lifestyle of some drinkers or drug users can make them vulnerable to many other problems such as socio-economic problems, legal problems, family and relationship problems. Alcohol or other drug use as a means of solving problems can sometimes relieve the immediate problems so that the individual does not attempt to develop or use alternatives. Two common types of problem-solving deficits are, firstly, not thinking through situations to evaluate the alternatives, and secondly, thinking that one has good problem-solving skills, but when confronted with a problem reacts impulsively. Problem-solving skills are not specific to drug-related behaviours, they are developed so that they can be adapted and applied to problems encountered in other areas of life. Often it is other problems encountered that result in the individual using drugs. Some people have a lot of problems or situations they consider to be problematic that they cannot avoid, for example family relationships.

Whatever the problem, it can be of benefit to take a systematic, planned approach to dealing with them. The technique described below is one which many people find helpful.

### *Aims of the topic*

- To help the client to identify problematic areas in his life and how he coped with them
- To increase awareness of the processes involved in problem solving by developing with the client a formulation of his ways of solving problems
- To discover how to work clearly and systematically in problem solving
- To identify the types of problems likely to be encountered in the future and practise some alternative responses.

### *Outline of the topic content and the techniques used*

***Discussion on the relevance of decision making and problem solving to substance misuse and relapse*** To facilitate discussion use information from the text above. An example of how to introduce the topic is given below:

***Example***

Dealing with problems is something that we all have to do throughout our lives. However, sometimes the problems that we face seem overwhelming and beyond solving. At such times, it can be of benefit to take a systematic, planned approach to dealing with them. The technique described below is one which many people find helpful. It basically involves breaking problems down into smaller parts and dealing with each in turn (give the handout in Appendix III for the client to look at whilst you work through each step).

These are the main steps:

- Identify your problems (and how you solve them)
  Some clients may not link their alcohol/drug use with other problem areas in their lives. In order to elucidate this it may be necessary to work back through some recent problems the client encountered. It is also important to identify situations where the client did use an alternative strategy successfully.

  To the client, it may seem that there is no single problem but many. If there is one single one, it can seem overwhelming and impossible to solve. Either way, the first step is for the client to list the problems they have. Be specific... for example 'I am unhappy' is probably made up of several different specific difficulties, perhaps 'My girlfriend and I argue a lot', 'I am worried about my Dad's ill-health', and 'I miss the contact with people that I used to have when at college'.

  In order to develop more effective strategies clients in addition need to have an understanding of their own pattern of responding in different problem areas. It may be that some of the issues that clients identify as problems are a result of their beliefs either about themselves or about the issue. Ask the client to elaborate if possible.

- Decide which problem is to be tackled first.
  It is best to focus on one of the problems on the list at first. This might not be the most central and pressing one for you, but it may be worth tackling an 'easier' one to start with, instead of tackling the more complicated problems headlong. More difficult problems can then appear to be more solvable as your confidence increases. For example, it may be better to concentrate on improving your social life rather than starting out trying to sort out relationship and family problems.

- Decide on your goal and set targets for yourself.
  What are your goals? For example, if you would like to improve your social life, what does this mean? Does it mean re-establishing links with old friends, making new ones, or doing both? What are your targets? Targets need to be SMART (specific, measurable, agreed, realistic, time limited). For example, one outing and one telephone call a week with any friend may be more achievable to start with than aiming to go to five evening classes a week.

- Work out the steps that are necessary to achieve your targets.
  Sometimes only one step will be required, sometimes more than one. It can help to brainstorm ideas, perhaps with another person. This involves generating as many potential solutions as possible, even if some of them seem stupid or unlikely.

Write them all down, and don't evaluate them until you have finished.

Then go through them and think about the advantages and disadvantages of each one in turn.

Decide from this which is the best option (or options).

Don't forget to take into account the resources that you have and don't be afraid to use them. For example, if you were nervous about going somewhere for the first time, it may be worth thinking about who might come with you.

- Work through the steps towards your goal.
  If you encounter difficulties along the way, it may be that steps are unmanageable and it may be worth thinking about whether you can break them down any further. When you do succeed, reward yourself! It may seem easy afterwards, but it is important to recognize what you have achieved.

### Practical example: Working through these stages

Having discussed the theory with the client, ask for a relatively simple but real example of a problem from the client. Next, go through each of the steps above using a real example and ensuring that the client, not you, takes responsibility for leading and doing most of the work (otherwise it could become a talk given by you which the client may not take on board or benefit from).

***Planning for future problems*** Finally, not all problems can be anticipated. Enabling the client to think ahead about forthcoming situations that could be problematic, and working through them using the problem-solving plan is a good exercise to encourage the client to plan and anticipate things.

#### *Out-of-session practise for this topic*

One possibility is for clients to monitor what problems they encounter each day and how they responded. A diary for this might be useful. Practise with the client how to use the diary.

Another exercise might be for clients to choose an example each day of a simple problem and to write their problem-solving thinking/process under the five headings in the handout used earlier.

This might then lead on to a third exercise; the client chooses a more complex and real problem, goes through the five steps described above with the therapist and sets each of the steps as a target to work towards between sessions. This may of course require a number of sessions or possibly combining discussion/feedback from this exercise into other, future, CBT topics.

## ▶ Core topic 7: Adapting lifestyle

#### *Introduction*

One of the problems that many drinkers and drug users have as we have noted before is that their whole lifestyle has become orientated around substances in one way or another. A lot of time and effort is put into being a heavy drinker or into obtaining and using drugs, such that when they stop using they find that they have a lot of time on their hands with nothing to do. Feelings of boredom and emptiness can inevitably lead to feeling alone and depression which can ultimately result in lapses and relapse. It is therefore important for the therapist to work with the client on these issues. This topic does not cover dealing with boredom (next core topic), which may be integral to making a lifestyle change and so needs to be considered. The present topic overlaps with other topics depending on the individual client, and elective sessions such as employment and job-seeking skills may be incorporated.



### *Aims of the topic*

- To identify aspects of the client's current lifestyle that are potentially counter-productive to treatment gains
- To start to develop a drug-free lifestyle.

### *Outline of the topic content and the techniques used*

***Discussion on the importance of lifestyle changes*** Use the information from the text above and get the views of the client. How relevant to them is this topic? Is a massive change in lifestyle needed or is the client's current lifestyle easily adapted to an alcohol/drug-free one?

*Steps towards a collaborative formulation*

- How does the client spend her time currently? This could be assisted by going through an activity schedule (see Chapter 3) in the session, asking about a typical but recent day (omitting mastery and pleasure ratings for this exercise).
- Does the client have a lot of spare time with nothing to do? If the client experiences this as boredom, leave further work on this for the next topic, but include here as part of the development of the formulation.
- What did the client enjoy or do before using drugs? 'What was life like before you started drinking heavily, how did you spend your time?'
- Does the client have a good network of non-alcohol/drug-using family and friends? Who is available to develop social activities that do not involve alcohol/drugs?
- If the majority of family and friends are alcohol/drug users – how can new contacts be made? Is it feasible to maintain contact with close friends who are drinkers/drug users without getting back into the network?
- With the client, identify the possible risks (e.g. depression, isolation, relapse) of not filling the vacuum of being a drinker/drug user.

***Developing a drug/alcohol-free lifestyle*** With the client, adopt the five steps from the problem-solving topic and use in this session to brainstorm how to build a new lifestyle. This can include:

- Looking at how the client spends her time using daily activity schedules completed between sessions and evaluating them.
- Challenge beliefs by exploring skills the client has, for example 'what is the point, I'm no good at anything?' can be challenged by looking at past successes, activities and skills shown in the past, or reframing of perception of current skills being used to maintain current drink/drugs lifestyle into transferable skills which can be adapted to a more positive lifestyle. An example of a reframing might be a drinker who manages to hold down a responsible job despite their drinking; the person clearly has skills and resources which without drinking would be even more fruitful. Or a heroin user who is homeless clearly has skills for surviving on the streets that could be used in a positive drug-free way.
- Brainstorming with the client to think of new ways to fill time, and continue the activity schedules and evaluate progress.
- Help the client to re-establish contact or improve contact with non-drinking or drug-using friends – this may involve exploring potential problems, for example, 'they think I'm scum, they won't want to see me', and rehearsing and practising getting in touch with them.
- What positive addictions might replace the problematic one? Is exercise/sport a possibility? Any other absorbing activities that could be seen as a positive addiction (craft work; attending self-help meetings, e.g. AA/NA)?

### *Out-of-session practise for this topic*

Possibilities include:

- Complete a pay-off matrix (see Appendix I, and as used in Topic 1) but instead of drug use, consider the benefits and disadvantages of making/not making a lifestyle change.
- Complete a change plan worksheet but instead of alcohol/drug use as the item to be changed, consider a lifestyle change area. Like objectives in previous sessions, make this specific, measurable, agreed, realistic, time limited and able to be broken into small steps to put into practise between sessions.
- Complete an activity schedule for the time between this and the next session.
- Identify goals and steps for achieving them with regard to a lifestyle change.
- Identify non-drinkers/drug users the client knows and outline an action plan of how to contact them or make better use of them (to mutual advantage of course).
- Plan to fill time with constructive/therapeutic activities that are not compatible with previous lifestyle.

## ▶ Core topic 8: Managing boredom

### *Introduction*

Boredom, emptiness and bereavement are problems that present a challenge for progress in treatment and longer term progress. Apart from generally helping the client to develop a drug-free lifestyle, this topic is focused on exploring boredom and the vacuum created by not being a drinker/drug user as specific barriers to progress.

As well as putting the client at risk of depression, which itself may be a high risk for relapse, for some substance misusers, a low tolerance for boredom drives them to pursue stimulation and excitement and may be part of the reason for becoming involved in their addiction. This may result in a belief system that revolves around the need to be constantly stimulated or having an altered mood and/or state of consciousness. Some clients experience emptiness, which can be a result of the loss of a lifestyle and things associated with it, and a lack of motivation to adapt. This topic involves two main strategies:

i. Construct new beliefs about boredom, using cognitive techniques.

ii. Overcome boredom, using activity scheduling.

### *Aims of the topic*

- To identify and challenge beliefs concerning the need for constant stimulation
- To explore and develop alternative activities for filling time/developing a new lifestyle specifically to overcome boredom
- To explore and develop the client's capacity to tolerate boredom and emptiness.

### *Outline of the topic content and the techniques used*

#### *Education on how to activate oneself*

**The problem**

Being bored, or having time on your hands that wasn't there before you started on this programme (getting money together, scoring or being intoxicated) or finding it hard to do things because you're feeling down, are common problems when people give up illicit drugs or heavy drinking. Inactivity is a vicious circle. It slows you down, mentally and physically. It makes everything an effort. Life seems tedious, with no fun. You tire easily. You do less, and may blame yourself for doing less. You might come to believe you can do nothing, and that you'll never get over it. That makes you more inactive or depressed. It becomes even more difficult to do anything. And so it goes on.

**The way out**

Becoming more active is one way to break the vicious circle.

- Activity helps prevent relapse. It occupies your mind away from drinking/using and fills your day, it makes you less lethargic, and may possibly even help you to sleep better at night.
- Activity makes you feel better. If nothing else, it takes your mind off your painful feelings. It gives you the sense that you are taking control of your life again, and achieving something worthwhile. You may even find there are things you enjoy, once you try them.
- Activity makes you feel less tired. Normally, when you are tired, you need rest. When you are bored or depressed, the opposite is true – you need to do more. Doing nothing will only make you feel more lethargic and exhausted.
- Activity motivates you to do more. In boredom and depression, motivation works backwards. The more you do, the more you feel like doing.
- Activity improves your ability to think. Once you get started, problems which appeared insoluble come into perspective.
- People who matter to you will probably be pleased to see you doing more.

**The difficulty**

In spite of these advantages, getting going again is not easy. This is sometimes because negative thoughts stand in your way. When faced with something you want to accomplish, you find yourself thinking 'I won't enjoy it', 'It's boring', 'I'll only make a mess of it', 'It's too difficult', and other similar negative thoughts. These thoughts will block you from taking action.

Later on, we (the therapist and client) will work directly on the thoughts which are stopping you from getting down to what you want to do, no matter how you try. Our aim will be for you to learn to notice and challenge them, so that they no longer stand in your way.

But first of all, our goal is to find out exactly what you are doing, and then build on what we discover.

***Activity schedules*** An activity schedule (see Chapter 3) is an hour-by-hour record of what a person does. It is a means of showing to the individual how he is in fact spending his time, and of helping him to plan the day enjoyably and productively. There are two steps involved:

*Step I: Self-monitoring* For the next few days, ask the client:

- To record exactly what she does, hour by hour. This can be done first of all in the session with the therapist – choose a recent typical day as an example. Use a blank schedule for the out-of-session exercise.

- To give each activity a rating between 0 and 10 for pleasure (*P*), and mastery or sense of achievement (*M*). $P = 0$ would mean that the client had not enjoyed an activity at all. $P = 10$ would mean that it had been extremely enjoyable. The client can use any number between 0 and 10 to indicate the degree of enjoyment or pleasure experienced. Similarly, $M = 0$ means no sense of achievement, and $M = 10$ a considerable sense of achievement. Again, the client can use any number between 0 and 10 to indicate the degree of mastery experienced.
- It is important to rate the activities for *P* and *M* at the time, not in retrospect. If the client waits until later, negative thoughts may cause the client to devalue what has been done. When people are depressed for example, negative and unpleasant events are more easily noticed and remembered. The good things are blotted out by a sort of global pessimism. The same sometimes happens in boredom. Immediate ratings will help the client to become sensitive to even small degrees of pleasure and mastery, which might otherwise go unnoticed.
- *M* should be rated according to how difficult the particular activity is for the client now, not for how difficult it was before the client started drinking/taking drugs or got depressed, or how difficult everyone else would find it. When an individual is quitting alcohol or stopping illicit drugs or feeling depressed, things which would normally be very easy become difficult, so it is important for clients to give credit to themselves when they achieve something.

The activity schedule will provide hard data on what the client is doing and enjoying, and so challenge the belief that nothing goes well. It is very likely that the client will discover that he is more active and competent than he assumed, and that he is enjoying himself more than he thought.

Even if not, the client will have valuable evidence at hand to help find out what is getting in the way.

*Step II: Planning ahead* The next step is to plan each day in advance, including the sort of activities which give the client a sense of enjoyment and mastery.

- Structuring time will allow the client to feel that he is taking control of his life again, and provide a sense of purpose.
- The framework the client gives to himself will prevent him from sinking into a swamp of minor decisions, and help him to keep going even when he is feeling bad.
- Once the day's activities are laid out in writing, they will seem less overwhelming. The day is broken down into a series of manageable units, rather than a long shapeless stretch of time which the client must somehow fill.

Practical hints to help the client keep to his schedule

- Set aside a particular time each evening to record what you have done during the day and to plan for tomorrow. Try to choose a time when you will not be interrupted, and where there are no other pressing demands on you.

- If you have difficulty getting down to a particular task, tell your muscles in detail what to do. Be specific with your instructions. 'Get on with it' is too vague. 'Legs, walk. Hand, pick up pen. Now write' will give you the impetus to begin. As soon as you have told yourself what to do, do it–don't allow any pause for doubts to creep in.
- Watch out for self-defeating thoughts. Write them down and answer them at once. Then act on the answers (see section on Thought blocks for instructions).
- Remove distractions. Turn off the television and take the phone off the hook.
- Avoid bed. Beds are for sleeping, not for retreating to during the day. If you need relaxation during the day, then plan to achieve it some other way (e.g. listening to music, reading).
- Reward yourself for what you have done. You might, for instance, set a kitchen timer to signal the time to start or end an activity. Put up signs around the house to remind you what you are supposed to be doing. Tell someone you live with that 7:30 is your time for planning the next day and get them to remind you if you get distracted.
- Give yourself encouragement. Start the day with an activity which will give you a sense of achievement and which you have a good chance of completing successfully.
- Try to balance your day evenly between pleasure and mastery.
- Stick to the pattern of activities which you have found most rewarding and fulfilling in the past – there's a good chance that once you get going, you will find it so again.

When a record is done advise the client to take time to examine it carefully and see whether he can identify any factors which led up to trouble spots. Some things to look out for include:

- trying to do too many things in the time available
- trying to do too many things at once
- trying to achieve perfection in everything
- trying to please everybody all the time.

*How to make the activity schedule a help rather than a hindrance*

- Be flexible.
  Your schedule is a guide, not a god. Something may happen (a friend comes to visit you without warning, for instance) to throw you off schedule. This is a point where

you might become discouraged and be tempted to give up. Don't. Just continue with the schedule when you can.

- Think of alternatives.
  Some of the activities you plan may depend on factors beyond your control (e.g. the weather, your car breaking down). Supposing, for instance, you have planned a trip to the park with your children, have something up your sleeve in case it rains.
- Stick to the general plan.
  If for some reason you are unable to do what you have planned at the time you planned it (you wanted to sort out the bedroom and ended up talking to your friends), don't go back and try and do it later. Move onto the next activity, and plan what you have missed for the next day. If you finish an activity sooner than planned, leave your next activity until it is time for it on the schedule, and fill in the gap with a pleasurable activity. Have a list of pleasurable activities handy so that you have something available to choose from.
- Schedule activities by the hour or half-hour.
  Don't be too specific or too general. Getting your life sorted out is too general. Listing every single thing you have to do to get yourself sorted is too specific. Find the happy medium. Experience will tell you how long each activity is likely to take.
- Plan for quantity, not quality.
  Write down the amount of time you are going to spend on a particular activity, not how much you are going to do in that time. How much you can do may depend on factors outside of your control (interruptions, mechanical failures) or on other problems (difficulty in concentrating, fatigue). If you tell yourself you must clean your entire room and you don't do it, you'll probably think of yourself as a failure and get discouraged. If you simply set yourself to clean for an hour, then how much you do is neither here nor there. Remember, if a thing's worth doing, it's worth doing badly.
- Stick to the task in hand.
  Your immediate goal is to stick to the schedule, not to get over your drink/drugs problem, boredom or depression. If you work steadily at becoming more active, you will eventually feel better. But don't expect to be cured of all problems after an hour's television or painting a door. If you do, you'll only disappoint yourself.
- Review at the end of each planned day.
  This will help you to see clearly what you are doing, what room there is for improvement, and what changes you might like to make in the pattern of your day. If you didn't manage to stick to your plan, you may well learn something valuable about why you have been finding it difficult to become more active. Ask yourself what the problem was, and what you might do about it in future. Did you feel too tired? Were you aiming too high? Were you blocked by negative thoughts? Did you plan too many *M* activities, and not enough pleasure and relaxation? You can learn from these experiences.

- Remember everything is an action.
  Sitting in a chair reading the paper is an activity. So is going to bed, or staring out of the window brooding. But they may not be the activities which will give you the most satisfaction.

***Practical tasks*** Inactivity, boredom and depression often lead people to put off practical tasks they need to carry out. The pile mounts, and they end up feeling completely overwhelmed.

The following are practical steps of where to start:

- Make a list of everything you have been putting off.
- Number the tasks in order of priority – which needs to be done first? If you can't decide, number them in alphabetical order. The important thing at this stage is to do something.
- Take the first task and break it down into small steps. What exactly do you have to do in order to complete it?
- Rehearse the task mentally, step by step. Write down any practical difficulties you may encounter, and work out what you will do about them.
- Write down any negative thoughts that come to you about doing the task, and answer them.
- Take the task step by step, dealing with difficulties and negative thoughts as they occur, just as you have practised mentally.
- Quit when you are winning, not when things are going badly. This will leave you feeling good about what you achieve and ready to carry on.
- As soon as you have finished, write down what you have done on your activity schedule, and rate it at once for *P* and *M*.
- Focus on what you have achieved, not on all the other things you still have to do. Watch out for negative thoughts which will make you devalue or discount what you have done. Write these thoughts down and answer them.
- Take the next task, and tackle it in the same way.

***Thought blocks to becoming more active*** When people are bored or depressed over long periods of time, it is their negative thinking that keeps them so. Most people get over this within a certain period. If they don't, there is sure to be some negative thinking going on, and keeping them down. The most powerful way to overcome inactivity is to identify negative thoughts as they occur, and to challenge them. Give some examples of the kind of thoughts that may be preventing a person from becoming more active, together with some possible answers to them. Emphasize that they are not the right answers, or the only answers – they are just some suggestions. Emphasize that with practise, the client will be able to find the answers that make sense.

*Example*

| Automatic negative thoughts | Possible answers |
|---|---|
| I can't do anything practical – there are too many practical difficulties. | There are always practical difficulties involved in doing anything - it's part of life. What would I do about them if I wasn't feeling the way I do just now? Is there anyone who could give me advice with those I don't know how to handle (e.g. counsellor, doctor)? |
| I can't keep a schedule - I've never been a record keeper. | Keeping written records is a skill that I can learn. I may not have done this before, but that doesn't mean to say I can't if I try. After all, I've used lists before, for shopping and to remember what to take on holiday. I could start by listing all the things I have to do. |
| There's too much to do - I can't cope. | Believing this is all part of the problem. If I write down what I need to do, it won't seem so overwhelming. I don't have to do it all at once. I can take things one at a time. |
| It's too difficult | It only seems difficult because of the way I'm feeling just now. I've done more difficult things than this in the past. |
| I won't know how to go about it | The idea is to have a go, not to produce the perfect performance. It's better to try and find out how I do, than not to do anything at all. |
| I don't want to | I don't now but I did earlier on. In any case, whether I want to is irrelevant. The point is, it would be better for me to do it. |
| I don't think I'm up to it just now - I'll wait 'til I'm feeling better | I won't know if I'm up to it until I try. If I wait 'til I feel like it, I'll never do it. Doing it will make me feel better. |

***Identify and challenge beliefs concerning the need for constant stimulation*** Explore the client's perception of the role of drugs in satisfying this need, so that a more balanced view of drugs as a means to resolve boredom can be adopted. This can be accomplished using techniques such as Socratic questioning, downward arrow exercises and advantages/disadvantages analysis.

***Explore and develop the client's capacity to tolerate boredom and emptiness*** It is not usually possible to be stimulated all of the time, so re-evaluating boredom and emptiness and developing ways of tolerating it is important. Reframing empty time into a positive experience may sound an impossible task, but a discussion around the possible benefits – time to recharge the batteries, an opportunity to give the body a rest, an opportunity to clear the mind – may be helped using a pay-off matrix (see

Appendix I) and asking Socratic questions following this. Behavioural experiments testing out the effects of tolerating boredom may also be devised.

### *Out-of-session practise for this topic*

Possibilities include:

- Completing a pay-off matrix (see Appendix I, Topic 1) but instead of drug use, consider the benefits and disadvantages of accepting boredom as a necessary part of life.
- Completing a change plan worksheet (Topic 1) but instead of alcohol/drug use as the item to be changed, consider how to get going with activities/pastimes that give pleasure and a sense of mastery.
- Complete an activity schedule in the way described above for the time between this and the next session (see Chapter 3).
- Choose one of the other exercises described above for activity scheduling, dealing with unhelpful thoughts/thought blocks, or building a behavioural experiment relevant to this topic.

## Core topic 9: Relapse prevention, maintenance of stability and ending treatment

### *Introduction*

Ending treatment is a time for the client and therapist to review the plans and goals of the treatment and the progress made. One of the goals throughout the treatment is for the therapist to enable clients to recognize their thought and behaviour patterns and to learn and use new more adaptive ways of coping with them. Highlighting the good and positive attributes of the client is also important. The overall aim is for clients to be able to practise and develop what they have learnt during therapy with generalization to situations and circumstances not necessarily directly covered in this programme. In order to make it more likely that this generalization will occur, it is important for the client to feel positive about the therapy and the way it finished (i.e. it was properly discussed with the client before the last session!). In addition, revisiting the most pertinent topics for the individual client is known to aid training and hopefully adds to the sense of self-efficacy as well as confirming what skills the client has acquired or strengthened during therapy.

### *Aims of the topic*

- To review the plans and goals of the treatment
- Therapist to give feedback on the therapist's view of client's progress
- Client to give feedback on most and least helpful aspects of treatment

- To set longer term objectives the client wishes to work towards outside therapy
- To plan an emergency 'fire drill' if things start to go wrong.



***Outline of the topic content and the techniques used***

***What was covered?*** The therapist should review with the client the original plans and goals made during the assessment. The minimum content of this programme assuming the client attended all the planned sessions will have been:

- Building and maintaining motivation for change
- Identifying stimulus conditions, emotions and thoughts, as well as triggers for craving
- Developing strategies to limit exposure to stimulus conditions
- Developing skills to manage cravings, emotions and thoughts without using drugs or alcohol
- Learning to cope with lapses
- Learning how to recognize, challenge and manage unhelpful or dysfunctional thoughts about substance misuse
- Develop an emergency plan for coping with high-risk situations when other skills are not working
- Learning to recognize how one is 'setting oneself up' to use substances
- Generating pleasurable sober activities and relationships, building a life worth living and attaining a lifestyle balance.

Show each of the above on a handout for the client to look at as you and the client summarize the content of each topic. Add any of the elective topics the client covered.

***Therapist's feedback*** The therapist should feedback to the client on the overall progress made, with emphasis on the positive, as well as highlighting areas that might warrant further attention. It is most important that this is done in the MI style discussed in Topic 1 (and not like feeding back the results of an exam!). This is the end of the treatment and the emphasis should be positive, but emphasizing the need to keep practising to maintain and improve what the client has already learned, as is the case with all newly learned skills.

***Client's feedback*** The therapist should ask the client to feedback his views of progress made and the aspects of the treatment he found most and least helpful. It is also a time for the therapist to elicit the client's concerns about what will happen when he leaves. Some clients become very dependent on the therapy session and think that they need it to maintain their progress. Again using the MI style referred to earlier for giving advice, clients can be given the message that progress relies on work done in their own environment without the need for professional help, that it is positive progress to be ending a programme and that in the longer term it is part of the normalization of their new way of living not to be in therapy!

***Longer term goal planning*** This can take the same change plan worksheet approach as was described in Topic 1 and will vary according to each individual's needs. The general principle, however, is that forethought is being given to what clients want their life to look like in future and what they might do to make this happen. The same principles for goal setting used earlier (i.e. steps need to be specific, measurable, agreed, realistic and time-limited) should be used. Encourage the client to focus on one area of change at a time unless the radical lifestyle change is the better option for that client.

***Emergency plan – what to do when things are going wrong*** Again this can take the form of a change plan worksheet but this time get the client to think about what to do when all else fails. This might include in the 'What is it that I want to change' box consideration of choice points/decision alternatives, the various routes that could be taken other than drinking/using again. In the 'Steps I plan to take in changing' box list the various options that will protect against drinking/using such as contacting a friend, revisiting the earlier topics, 'do your activity that buys you (personally) time, get yourself into a situation where you can't drink, fill yourself with food', or whatever it is that the therapist and client can devise as the client's 'escape route' from lapsing. In the box on who can help, again be specific and ensure the client has contact and other details.

### *Out-of-session practise for this topic*

As this is the final session the practise should be of the topic identified in the feedback as needing further strengthening. A handout of topics covered could be offered to the client and another change plan worksheet completed for the client to work on after therapy. This can be done in this session with the area identified for action/change being agreed mutually between therapist and client and if possible practised in the session.

CHAPTER SEVEN

# Elective topics

## Introduction

### *Why elective topics?*

The core topics presented in the previous chapter cover issues/concepts/factors which are common to all clients, and according to the theoretical model presented here, must be addressed in therapy in order to facilitate change in addictive behaviour. The amount and intensity of treatment required and how these factors interact with each other will vary across clients. However, clients may also vary in ways which are not causally related on a theoretical level with either the addiction or the recovery process (i.e. depression, anxiety, low self-esteem). There are, in addition, a number of problem behaviours which are common in substance misuse clients (i.e. criminal behaviour, issues of compliance with treatment). Such problem behaviours can interrupt or inhibit therapy process and progress. It may therefore be necessary to address them in the course of the therapeutic programme. This has to be achieved in a way which is compatible with cognitive-behaviour theory and practice.

In order to facilitate this, the elective topics presented in this book can be incorporated into individual therapy programmes in addition to the core topics. This means that the treatment can be tailored to the needs of individual clients. In this chapter, we present a number of elective topics which cover co-morbid conditions, as well as common problems encountered in substance misuse clients. Remember that not all elective topics are relevant to all clients.

### *How to choose the elective topics required*

We can generalize that the process of choosing elective topics has five steps.

1. Identify related problems that the client presents with.
2. Decide whether the problem can become an elective topic.
3. Decide when the elective topic is going to be incorporated into the programme.
4. Decide how many sessions are required.
5. Decide when there is a need for onward referral.

Problems that can be addressed within an elective topic can be identified at different times during treatment. The most common time points are:

- *Assessment*: the client may present from the beginning with a list of problems which are related to substance misuse directly or indirectly. The therapist should allocate time to explore each one of them. The aim is to explore the interaction between all presenting problems and how: (a) they should be incorporated into the case formulation; and (b) they relate to the substance misuse model.

***Example***

A 40-year-old lady presents with a drinking problem as well as an eating problem, compulsive cleaning and chronic low mood. Detailed assessment reveals that eating difficulties (starvation) and compulsive cleaning were related to the experience of abuse in childhood, and later on to violence within her first marriage. Both were used as avoidance behaviours (avoidance of memories). Alcohol use served a similar function; it helped to reduce overall levels of anxiety and insecurity, as well as anxiety resulting from the inability to perform the above avoidance behaviours when she was in a very low mood. The latter was also frequently associated with the recollection of traumatic experiences, but it was also the result of alcohol misuse, and predisposed to further use and the spiralling of the model.

At the later stages of assessment, or even at the development of the formulation, other problems may become apparent. The therapist at this point needs to explore such problems and how they are connected with substance misuse.

- *During the core topic sessions*: it is often the case that new issues emerge in the course of addressing core topics. The most common of these is in working with stimulus conditions. As per definition, they can include external or internal states such as boredom, anxiety and low mood. Sometimes, stimulus conditions require a more extensive assessment and treatment outside of the sessions related to the core topic 'Identifying stimulus conditions'. Another common example is the emergence of low self-esteem as an elective topic from the assertiveness training topic. If necessary, the therapist can incorporate such problems into the cognitive case formulation and the substance misuse model. It is clear from the above that whenever a problem or issue appears to require more detailed attention than what can be offered as part of the core topic (independently of the number of sessions allocated) then it is better to include an elective topic on this problem.
- *Recurrent issues during treatment*: sometimes problem behaviours such as criminal behaviour, risk behaviours, childcare issues or other crisis can interfere with the treatment. The therapist should then offer separate sessions to explore such issues. Here again, the therapist should aim to understand recurrent problems using the cognitive formulation and model of addiction.

The decision about when to add the elective topic is one that should be taken collaboratively with the client, and it will depend on the progress in treatment. It is advisable to add elective topics on problems identified during assessment in a planned way, usually after completion of the core topic sessions. For problems identified and/or directly related to core topics, it may be beneficial to add the relevant elective topic as an extension of the core topic.

The number and emphasis of the sessions required will be based on the individual case formulation. When the number of sessions required for elective topics is more than that required for the related core topic, onward referral to other professionals or services for the management of the identified problem might be indicated. This is particularly important for co-morbid disorders. Addiction therapists should be focused on treating the addiction problem. When a problem needs more detailed attention than what can be offered as an elective topic within the addiction model, then referral to another professional is required.



### *How to use elective topics*

The use of elective topics should follow two main principles:

1. Problem topics should be included in the case formulation (if identified early), or at later stages, the case formulation should be modified to include them. In other words, it is necessary that the therapist uses cognitive theory to understand the content and relationship of problems/topics with substance misuse.
2. Elective topics should fit the model in the same way as the core topics fit the model. The therapist should be concerned with the role or function of this problem/topic to the spiralling of the model. Is it a stimulus condition, does it increase positive expectancies, does it affect the ability to take the right decision when exposed to a stimulus condition and so on?

As with the cognitive-behavioural treatment of other psychological problems, the focus should be on management of the symptoms, for example exploring with the client alternative, more functional ways of understanding and coping with the symptoms. In the case of co-morbid disorders (i.e. depression), it is advised that the therapist consult/review the relevant cognitive models. Clinicians in the addiction field have diverse training and may be familiar with terminology other than the cognitive-behavioural one. Inexperienced therapists have the tendency to revert to and use familiar old ways to deal with challenging problems. We strongly advise therapists not to abandon cognitive theory and terminology. It is usually more effective to use one theory to understand and treat a client rather than picking and mixing different concepts and terms. The so-called eclectic approaches carry the great risk of an unstructured, atheoretical and confusing treatment for both client and therapist.

The elective topics presented in detail here should be used as a guide for dealing with any similar problems. Some of these topics cover co-morbid disorders and others cover problems common to clients with substance misuse.

## ▶ Elective topic 1: Mood disorders – depression

### *Introduction*

Depression is extremely common in substance misusers attending treatment (Weaver *et al.*, 2003). The management of clients with this co-morbidity may be challenging. Depressed individuals are often reluctant to seek help in the earlier stages of the disorder, before some of their negative cognitive–affective behavioural patterns have strengthened. They often label themselves as 'weak' or 'failures'. This is even more so the case with individuals who use substances to self-medicate. The added stigma and often judgemental attitude of health professionals can have a major adverse impact on the individual and motivation to ask for help. Therapists should be aware of the increased probability of co-morbidity, and the risks and consequences to the individual and their environment. Parallel treatment by mental health and substance misuse services is far from ideal, therefore the addiction therapist should be able to address symptoms of depression within the substance misuse treatment.

### *Cognitive-behavioural model of depression*

According to Beck's (1976) cognitive specificity hypothesis, depressed clients have a different cognitive profile from those with other psychiatric problems, showing primarily themes of loss, defeat, failure in their cognitive content and a systematic negative bias. Beck paid attention to the 'negative cognitive triad' in depressed clients: a tendency to view themselves, the future and their experience around them almost entirely in negative terms. Beck argued that the worldview of depressed clients contributes to maintaining most of the symptoms, as well as interfering with effective management of real-life problems. The first task for the cognitive therapist is to increase the client's awareness of the way in which they interpret their experiences and to discover the adaptiveness or maladaptiveness of such constructions. The next task is to explore and learn to utilize other more adaptive ways of understanding experience.

Beck's cognitive model of depression proposes that people develop negative core beliefs about themselves as a result of adverse early experiences. Using drugs may have developed as a compensatory strategy in an attempt to find some relief in what seemed like a hopeless situation. It is these beliefs that affect the individual's view of themselves, their immediate situation and the future.

### *Assessment and formulation*

Symptoms of depression may be identified in the assessment or they may come up later in the course of treatment. Awareness of depressive symptoms is important because they will ultimately affect the progress and prognosis of treatment. The assessment should aim to establish the relationship between substance misuse and symptoms of depression.

- Are there stimulus conditions common to depression and substance use?
- Is depression an internal stimulus condition for drug use?
- Is depression a consequence of drug use? Is shame and/or guilt associated with depression?
- Does depression affect the client's ability to engage in treatment? Should the emphasis be on treating depression before drug use? Are there strong suicidal tendencies that warrant intervention and precaution?

Kuehlwein (2002) proposed that a basic conceptualization of depression needs to cover the following areas:

- Major current problems (including behavioural, cognitive, affective and physiological) that the client is experiencing. The therapist needs to gather a list of current problems and goals and help the client to define them as clearly as possible.
- Examples of situations in which such problems occur should be noted.
- Current predisposing events and situations.
- Any metaphors, images or dreams the client reports that represents important aspects of the problem concerned.
- Cognitive, affective, physiological and behavioural strategies that the client appears to employ as coping attempts. This should include alcohol or drug misuse.
- Early experiences, especially those that had a large impact on the client in childhood, or disturbing events later in life that possibly affected the meaning-making structures at the time.
- Past situations of good coping during stress or change.
- Past accomplishments.
- Interests and hobbies. These can be used by the therapist as a source to challenge dysfunctional beliefs.
- Past and present people that have had a positive impact on the client.

### *Intervention*

Symptom relief early in treatment is crucial to engage clients. Most substance misuse clients who suffer from depression present feeling distressed. By introducing the idea that problems primarily result from the dysfunctional interpretations of situations, rather than the situations themselves, the therapist can help the client to view their problem as one which has possible solutions rather than being hopelessly insoluble.

Kuehlwein (2002) proposed that the treatment model of depression can be divided into three stages. The addiction therapist should not use the whole depression model, but when it has been decided to include one or more sessions to address symptoms of depression, it might be useful to know the three stages, and chose what needs to be incorporated in the client's treatment plan:

1. Define and prioritize target problems, increase hope, educate the client in the cognitive-behavioural model and clarify the relationship between beliefs, affect and behaviour.
2. Teach the client about cognitive distortions; identify, evaluate and modify dysfunctional cognitions; test accuracy of targeted beliefs using life examples; refine and practise social skills and problem-solving strategies. The therapist and client first work on the superficial level of dysfunctional automatic thoughts. They explore concrete, specific time-limited situations in current life, and as they gather more information about affect, behaviour and cognitions, they build an individualized and flexible formulation of how situations, behaviours, emotions, physical symptoms and cognitions fit together. This enables the client to see beliefs as beliefs and not as truth.
3. Elicit, examine and modify deeper cognitive structures (conditional assumptions and core beliefs) and work on relapse prevention. During this stage, therapist and client look for themes across major automatic thoughts and in particular, those that are most closely tied to distressing affect.

In most cases, the client may also have other more adaptable beliefs which are currently overshadowed by the stronger dysfunctional attitudes, triggered by the client's depressive mood. With the use of Socratic questioning, the therapist should help the client to uncover, appreciate and strengthen such beliefs. Repetition of positive beliefs using flashcards will help the client to re-enforce new/or old adaptive beliefs.

Several behavioural or cognitive techniques that have already been presented in Chapter 3 can be used to modify depressive symptoms. However, the therapist should be aware that clients can be very sensitive to criticism, and can feel easily rejected or inadequate.

Sometimes, automatic thoughts can occur in imagined form. These internal pictures can appear very real because in some senses they actually see their fears being realized, or can relive past traumatic experiences. Using visualization the client can be taught to replace those images with more accurate adaptive mental images.

Activity planning and scheduling is very helpful in early stages to enable clients to become more active, and experiment with the possible positive effects on their mood. It also facilitates control over dysphoria, improves confidence and challenges beliefs about helplessness. Graded task assignments are helpful when clients feel overwhelmed by the perceived tasks and burdens of life.

An important cognitive strategy is to help the client with meta-cognition (think about thinking), to examine and establish what actually happened in order to distinguish between this and what they think has happened. Helpful tools in this strategy are the daily thought record and Socratic questioning.

Frequently, clients complain that they know that the new beliefs are appropriate, but the old beliefs still 'feel' more accurate. Rational–emotional role-play is the ideal intervention to help such clients. Rational–emotional role-play uses the basic structure of the behavioural technique of role-play. To start with, the client identifies two opposing beliefs: one emotionally persuasive and maladaptive; and one intellectually persuasive and more adaptive. The client changes chairs, and the therapist encourages the client to verbalize all the data used over the years to support the old core belief. At the next stage, the client returns to the original chair and with prompting or modelling, argues against the alleged evidence previously offered.

### *Suicidal risk*

Most clients arrive at the option of suicide after many other attempts to solve their problems. It is very important for the therapist dealing with a suicidal client to elicit the client's reasons both for and against this drastic option. This ensures that both of the client's important perspectives are heard and understood.

For more details on this subject see Kuehlwein (2002) and Greenberger and Padesky (1995).

## Elective topic 2: Worry and anxiety

### *Introduction*

The co-morbidity between anxiety and substance misuse has been reported to be very high (Weaver *et al.*, 2003). Anxiety can predispose an individual to drinking or drug taking as a form of self-medication, and/or in turn drinking or drug taking can perpetuate anxiety. Therefore, it is very important that levels of anxiety and their relationship to substance misuse are assessed and incorporated into the CBT treatment plan for the substance misuse problem.

### *Cognitive-behavioural model for worry and Generalised Anxiety Disorder (GAD)*

According to cognitive-behavioural theory, the symptoms of GAD result from the spiralling of longstanding and inflexible cognitive and physiological responses to a constantly perceived threat. Cognitive-behavioural interventions aim to provide coping skills, which in turn facilitate the development of a flexible and adaptive lifestyle which will reduce the experience of anxiety. Clients suffering from GAD have a tendency to make inaccurate negative interpretations which remain uncorrected by their positive experiences. CBT teaches clients to actively correct inaccurate negative interpretations by paying attention to the real-life evidence.

### *Assessment and formulation*

Assessment of worry and anxiety should include a list of current situations that precipitate anxiety. Clients very often report constant anxiety, but feel unable to identify specific episodes. Specific examples of recent experience can provide detailed information that can help to unfold the cycle of anxiety, and be used as educational material. Functional analysis of current experiences is also very important. Assessment should also include a list of all possible threats that the individual considers realistic, and the evidence for them. Formulation for GAD should include early experiences that might have predisposed the individual to perceive the environment as threatening and him/herself as hopeless to deal effectively with it.

### *Intervention*

Clients are informed that worry is a result of habits from the past, and that therapy is focused on teaching new skills. New cognitive or behavioural techniques should be introduced and practised during the session in order to create an immediate and even small positive effect. The more confidence clients have in a technique, the more motivated they will be to practise it, and the more effective it will be. Here, we outline some important techniques:

- **(a)** Self-monitoring and early cue detection: constant self-monitoring of anxiety cues is the foundation for the CBT treatment of GAD. Early internal or external cues typically lead to an upward spiralling of anxiety. The goal of therapy is to change the client's response to their own reactions to the cues and to strengthen new coping responses. Self-monitoring can help clients to identify and pay attention to other emotions, such as anger, frustration and depression. It is important that the client records information at the time it happens. The therapist can help the client to develop ways to create reminders in their environment.
- **(b)** Stimulus control methods: stimulus control techniques can help the client reduce the association between worry and the identified specific cues, which in turn can reduce the intensity and frequency of the worry response. The first step is to schedule a daily 30-minute period during which the client will worry. This period should occur at the same time and place every day, and should not be associated with work or relaxation. The client has to postpone worrying at all other times and places until the scheduled 30-minute period and focus the attention on what is going on in the environment. If they find it very difficult to control or postpone worry, they should go immediately to the designated 'worry' spot, and worry intensively until their worry is under control. Then they are allowed to return to their previous activity.
- **(c)** Relaxation methods are used to increase autonomic flexibility.
- **(d)** Another approach focuses on modification of the negative interpretation and predictions that the individual generates from neutral information. The first step is for clients to identify the thoughts, images, beliefs that create anxiety. They are then treated like hypotheses rather than facts and evidence is gathered to support or refute their thoughts. They can also estimate the probability that the feared outcome will actually happen, using the experience of how frequently it has happened in the past.

**(e)** Distancing is a very useful method, which is easer to use for learning how to logically analyse thoughts. The client works with the thoughts and predictions of another person rather than themselves. First they gather all evidence, then they examine it carefully to determine whether the original thought was accurate and finally they try to come up with multiple alternative interpretations that are less anxiety provoking, and equally or more likely truly based on the evidence they have.

**(f)** Two rules are important to help clients determine how accurate are their views: (i) they should avoid only probable dangers rather than every outcome. One helpful way to illustrate this point is by describing what life might be like if people worried about everything that could happen; (ii) they should suspend judgement until they have enough evidence to support a particular conclusion. An advantages/disadvantages analysis might be helpful.

De-catastrophizing (a version of downward arrow exercise, in which you explore the worst fears of the client and aim to put them in perspective) and behavioural experiments are very helpful techniques for reducing the impact of worrying thoughts. The therapist should help the client to generate their own multiple alternative perspectives, rather than convincing them to believe something that does not feel true. It is important for the therapist to be as flexible as possible.

For more details on this subject see Newman and Borkovec (2002).

## Elective topic 3: Low self-esteem

### *Introduction*

It is a common clinical experience that many clients in treatment for a substance misuse problem have low self-esteem. This can be even more so the case with those who are aware of their substance problem, but are not accessing treatment. Low self-esteem can also interact with substance use and have a major impact on treatment progress at different levels. Low self-esteem is not a psychiatric diagnosis per se. It is not a clinical condition or a personality disorder as conceptualized in the existing diagnostic systems. It can be a background difficulty which accompanies or underlies more precisely definable presenting problems.

### *Cognitive-behavioural model of low self-esteem*

Melanie Fennell (1998) proposes that low self-esteem can be understood as a generic cognitive representation of the self, which is derived from specific experiences, and which guides subsequent information processing and behaviour. In this way it shapes the everyday thoughts, feelings and behaviour of the individual, which in turn are maintained and reinforced by the associated ongoing biases in cognitive processing and maladaptive behaviour, and therefore resistant to change. Low self-esteem may be seen as a learned, negative, global judgement about the self. It can be seen as a 'core belief' which might be the basis for a wide range of other short-term or long-term problems.

### *Assessment and formulation*

The model suggests that the global negative belief about the self forms the 'bottom line'. Since the 'bottom line' is perceived to be true, individuals develop conditional assumptions, principles and standards against which they measure self-worth and have requirements which they must meet in order to maintain self-esteem. Problems arise in situations where the person either fails or might fail to achieve the standards specified by the assumptions. The model suggests that in situations where the individual is uncertain about the ability to meet the standards s/he develops anxiety followed by depression.

Detailed assessment of how low self-esteem interacts with substance misuse is essential. Assessment of early life experiences that led to the 'bottom line' is crucial. How relevant are such experiences to substance misuse? Is for example low self-esteem related core beliefs activated when the client faces a stimulus condition? Or is low self-esteem and the associated depression an internal stimulus condition that makes the client vulnerable to relapse? Do low self-esteem beliefs colour permissive beliefs and lead to substance use as a safety behaviour?

### *Intervention*

As already discussed above, the role of low self-esteem can vary in its impact and severity. For some clients, it can be an aspect or a consequence of the substance misuse problem, and can be resolved directly as the client is successfully addressing his drug or alcohol problem without any specific intervention. This is more often the case with long-term drinking or drug abuse, and might be the result of several previous unsuccessful attempts to control use or have treatment. Control over substance misuse or successful steps in treatment of substance misuse might improve self-esteem. Sometimes, basic education about the process of substance misuse, of treatment and sharing of formulation and expectation from treatment can have a positive impact on self-esteem, and can modify the meaning that the client has attributed to previous treatment failures. It can also be an aspect of another associated problem, such as depression or anxiety, and treatment of such problems (as presented in the above elective topics) can resolve low self-esteem too.

When and how many sessions will be required will depend on formulation, and on the experience of the therapeutic interaction with the client during the assessment sessions. In general, the therapist might need a session to assess the impact of low self-esteem early in treatment as it might affect interaction during the sessions, the ability of the client to benefit from between-session practice or overall compliance with the treatment programme. The results of the assessment might guide and influence the overall treatment approach, for example, how to set the agenda, put more emphasis on graded task assignment or emphasize positive achievements with relevant positive re-enforcements. Further session(s) may be required to address specific aspects of a low self-esteem problem. Here, we present the main steps of a treatment programme proposed by Melanie Fennell (1998) , which can be adapted according to the formulation to meet the needs of the specific client. In summary, interventions are designed to: (i) change the 'bottom line'; (ii) revise current guidelines for living; and (iii) to change thinking, affect and behaviour on a day-to-day basis.



**(i)** *Changing the 'bottom line'*: the therapist needs to find out whether experiences associated with the 'bottom line' are open to reinterpretation. The therapist encourages the client to search for counter-evidence, to record positive data and with this supportive evidence to attempt to establish a balanced view and realistic self-acceptance. This helps the client to break down dogmatic views and replace them with continuous hypotheses. It is important to help the client realize that beliefs about self are opinions and not facts.

**(ii)** *Revise current guidelines for living*: explore standards that would be more realistic and helpful. It is important to link the past with the present, and the experience with affect.

**(iii)** *Change thinking, affect and behaviour on a daily basis*: ask the client to monitor negative automatic thoughts and to search for evidence to use against them. Identify thinking errors, and challenge black and white thinking. Use weekly activity schedules to develop skills and strengths. Set realistic goals. Carry out and record behavioural experiments, or do imagery work with day-to-day issues. Use role-play to rehearse and enhance new or existing skills.

Do not forget to encourage the client to persist in particular when the change is slow and variable. Pay attention to the therapeutic relationship and your own thoughts and beliefs about the client as they can be strongly affected by the client's low self-esteem, and therefore impede treatment progress.

For more details on this subject see Melanie Fennell (1998).

## Elective topic 4: Anger, aggression and impulse control

### *Introduction*

Anger and its consequences constitute a great problem for individuals and society as a whole. Anger may be the precursor for social problems such as violent offending (including homicide), domestic violence and sexual offending. Anger and poor impulse control present as frequent problems in the lives of substance misusers. Low frustration tolerance frequently results in the individual responding to situations such as disappointments, hurt and imperfect behaviour of others with emotional overreactions. Use of substances can exaggerate this already existing reaction.

### *Cognitive-behavioural model for anger, aggression and impulse control*

Recent models of cognitive theory put emphasis on the process of appraisal and cognitive biases affecting the attribution of meaning to life events. According to these models, anger is the result of the symbolic meaning attached to the event, the cognitive mechanism involved in magnifying its impact and the degree of responsibility attributed to the other person. Low frustration tolerance (LFT) is one of the personality characteristics of people with impulse control difficulties which is exaggerated by substance misuse. The typical client with LFT goes through life judging situations in terms of the following: 'Am I getting what I want?', or 'Are people getting in my way?' Such clients look for immediate reinforcement or help. Dichotomous thinking like 'It is now or never' is a common cognitive error. By acting in an aggressive way, the client is able to neutralize the sense of powerlessness activated by the delay in gratification. The expression of hostility shifts the self-concept from 'I'm helpless' to 'I do have power'.

### *Assessment and formulation*

The assessment of aggressive and other impulsive acts should cover two main areas: environment and personal aspects.

- Environment includes: triggers (including background stressors); buffer factors such as good relationships, family support, achievement in some area; disinhibitors (alcohol, drugs); and short- and long-term consequences for both the perpetrator and others (peer group pressure or institutional reinforcement, e.g. respect by the peer group).
- Personal aspects include: biases in appraisal of life events, underlying beliefs and values supporting aggression; emotions preceding aggressive acts, such as anger or fear; problem-solving and overall coping skills.

The relationship between substance misuse and aggression should be explored in detail: Is substance misuse a disinhibitor, or is substance misuse perceived as a suppressor of impulsivity or aggression? The latter is a common belief strongly held by individuals with criminal records or aggressive behaviours earlier in their lives, who are currently seeking help for a substance misuse problem.

### *Intervention*

The first task in work with anger is to describe the problem behaviour that needs to be addressed. Typically, anger is the precursor of some act of aggression. Identifying triggers, using a similar approach to the core topic 'Identifying and dealing with stimulus conditions' is a crucial task. Practise during the session using techniques such as role-play and imagery in which, firstly, the client's behaviour in a specific situation is examined (e.g. identifying physical sensations or other cues that precede impulsive behaviour), and then appropriate reactions such as self-instruction are modelled by the therapist, and practised by the client.

Cognitive restructuring is another important aspect of CBT work. The main aim is for the client to switch from an impulsive to a reflective style, or to use coping skills already practised to deal with impulse control. The therapist and client need to identify, challenge and modify the biases in information processing that predispose the client towards anger. The therapist also needs to assess the rules and principles underlying the client's actions and reduce the rigidity with which these rules are applied. A third important area is what the client is striving to achieve in life. Sometimes social approval is his/her main goal because the client finds it very difficult to tolerate criticism. Therefore the client might select a social environment in order for his behaviour to be reinforced and accepted and avoid certain other social groups (i.e. family).

Practise outside sessions (as with any other topic) should be encouraged. Flashcards are very helpful for implementing cognitive restructuring and new coping strategies. Self-instruction could include statements like: 'Slow down, wait a minute', 'Don't act right away', 'Let me figure out what I have to do before I act' or a series of statements that would enable the client to understand the mechanics of his/her behaviour, and to explore alternative paths of action.

For more details on this subject see Howells (1998).

## Elective topic 5: Trauma and abuse

### *Introduction*

Survivors of traumas experience several psychological problems. A traumatic experience may lead to a diagnosis of post-traumatic stress disorder (PTSD), but the presence of psychological difficulties is not only related to the above diagnosis. Substance misuse, mood and anxiety disorders, personality changes, as well as problems with anger, rage and aggression are very common. Alcohol misuse problems have been reported in survivors of sexual abuse (Moncrieff *et al.*, 1996), survivors and perpetrators of violent trauma (Norton and Morgan, 1989), combat trauma (Sutker *et al.*, 1994) and disaster trauma (Green *et al.*, 1992). In a recent study, Reynolds *et al.* (2005) suggested that the prevalence of co-morbid PTSD and substance use disorder (SUD) was 38.5 % for current PTSD and 51.9 % for lifetime PTSD in a population receiving inpatient treatment for substance misuse. Traumatic experiences were highly prevalent in this population. A high percentage of the clients reported a specific connection between their traumatic experience and their drug use. In a similar study with a community sample, Reynolds *et al.* (2006) found a relationship between trauma and drug use, although the nature of this relationship was unclear. US studies have shown that concurrent treatment of trauma and substance dependence is associated with improved outcome (Ouimette *et al.*, 2000).

### *Cognitive-behavioural model of trauma and abuse*

Several authors have proposed a learning theory model for trauma and PTSD based on Mowrer's two-factor theory. According to this model, avoidance behaviours, including avoidance of reminders of the trauma and detachment from others, develop as a response to the anxiety associated with the reminders and they are reinforced by the resulting reduction in arousal. The persistence and generalization of avoidance behaviours contribute to broader deficits in functioning and can maintain the debilitating symptoms. Other theories are based on cognitive and information-processing models. These models propose that trauma influences how an individual appraises the world, themselves and others, and provides specific predictions with regard to behavioural and cognitive changes that occur when the individual interacts with the environment. Although these theories have been helpful in understanding post-trauma reactions, they have so far made a limited contribution to treatment interventions.

### *Assessment and formulation*

The experience of trauma or repeated traumas, particularly early in life can have a major impact in the development of core beliefs related to the client's views of self and the world. Core beliefs might be associated with low self-esteem and self-reproach. Traumatic reminders precipitate anxiety that the client often feels unable to control or cope with. The client therefore tries to either avoid reminders or block their effect (anxiety). Misuse of substances has proved to be one of the most effective ways of blocking unpleasant feelings or memories. Therefore traumatic reminders can be stimulus conditions precipitating relapse. Sometimes, long-term exposure to anxiety symptoms or withdrawal symptoms that resemble anxiety can reduce the client's tolerance and coping, and precipitate a need for avoidance. Substance use can be powerful avoidance behaviour. Therefore, exposure to internal or external stimuli can activate negative automatic thoughts related to the trauma, and lead to avoidance behaviour and use. Avoidance and detachment can also affect the therapeutic relationship (detachment) or the client's ability to undertake between-session practice. This is more prominent when practice includes behavioural experiments and exposure. As a general rule, the therapist should develop, as part of the formulation, simultaneous hypotheses to account for the complex interrelations of symptoms, problems and a variety of maintaining factors. The treatment plan should be a series of single treatment experiments following one hypothesis, results should be reviewed, and formulation and hypothesis should be modified accordingly.

### *Intervention*

It was emphasized above that CBT models for trauma put anxiety precipitated by reminders and avoidance of those reminders at the centre of the case formulation. Simple treatment models involve: (i) direct therapeutic exposure (e.g. desensitization, flooding, prolonged exposure) and (ii) anxiety management training.

- Therapeutic exposure requires the client to directly confront traumatic cues and/or memories within the therapy. The client repeatedly goes through the events of the trauma either imaginably and/or verbally. For this exposure to be effective, the client has to relive the traumatic events emotionally, access the meaning that has been attributed to the experience and challenge the response that has been established over the years. In this way the anxiety can be reduced and the cognitive appraisal of the traumatic events can be modified.

- Anxiety management training is a term that describes a number of interventions aiming to improve the client's ability to cope with anxiety symptoms. Typical skills include muscle relaxation (physical symptoms), role-playing (behavioural symptoms) and guided self-dialogue (cognitive symptoms).

The above simple approaches are based on the concept that anxiety is central to the client's impairment. This might not be the case when other problems are important and the clinical presentation can be very complicated when substance misuse is present. The above simple treatment models or a combination of the same can be helpful to the addiction clinician, and can easily be incorporated into the treatment plan as part of elective sessions. A more elaborated treatment model for adult trauma survivors is the phasic model, which has six phases: (i) the emotional and behavioural stabilization phase, which focuses on management of the crisis that initiates the client entering treatment (for trauma or PTSD) with the aim of enhancing the client's basic skills to meet basic needs and remain safe; (ii) the trauma education phase; (iii) the stress management phase (as above); (iv) the trauma focus phase uses exposure-based techniques (as above); (v) the relapse prevention phase is very similar to the relapse prevention strategies for substance abuse; and (vi) the follow-up phase. It is possible that the addiction therapist can incorporate aspects of these phases into the overall treatment plan as part of the elective sessions, whereas other phases can be covered through the core topic sessions of the addiction model.

For more detailed cover of how to treat complex cases of PTSD and trauma see Kimble, Riggs and Keane (1998).

## Elective topic 6: Relationship problems

### *Introduction*

The role of family members and significant others is very important in the treatment and recovery of clients with substance misuse problems. Extensive relationship and family support may be available, for example family support group, narcotic families or more specific couples/family therapy outside the service network.

Substance misusers are frequently part of substance misusing families, or are in relationships with other substance misusers (partners or close friends). This can pose either an external high-risk situation (substances easily available in the home environment or forming a significant part of the relationship), or an internal high-risk situation (difficult/abusive/stressful relationship) where drugs are used to relieve unpleasant emotional states as a result of relationship conflict. On the other hand, family/relationships with non-users may be a facilitator of treatment outside of the session. This may include discussing drug-related thoughts, supporting behavioural experiments, support in lifestyle adaptation and facilitating out-of-session exercises. It is important to assess the family's understanding and anxieties about the client's substance misuse problem in order to make a distinction between adaptive and maladaptive support strategies. The aim is to maintain a balance between emphasizing the role of the family's support, and also maintaining the client's autonomy. The elective topic presented below could be longer in duration than the typical treatment sessions.

### *Cognitive-behavioural model for couples and family problems*

Early behavioural treatment approaches placed emphasis on social exchange and contingency contracting with couples, and later emphasized communications training.

Cognitive-behaviour therapy with couples aims at: (a) modification of unrealistic expectations in the relationship; (b) correction of faulty attributions in relationship interactions; and (c) the use of self-instructional procedures to decrease destructive interactions.

Individuals develop their basic beliefs about relationships and how couples should interact early in life. Learning sources can be parents, culture and morals, the media and early dating experiences. Beliefs may exist as vague concepts of what relationships should be. Unrealistic expectations about relationships can reduce satisfaction and promote dysfunctional responses. Cognitive distortions may be evident in the automatic thoughts that couples report and may be uncovered with Socratic questioning regarding the meaning that a partner attaches to a specific event. Spouses' automatic thoughts about their interactions with one another commonly include inferences about the causes of pleasant and unpleasant events that occur between them.

### *Assessment and formulation*

Dattilio (2002) proposed that assessment should include assessment of each partner's standards on: (a) the nature of boundaries between partners; (b) distribution of control; and (c) partners' levels of instrumental and expressive investment in their relationship. Other aspects of relationship functioning should also be included such as leisure activities, career and job issues, household tasks and management and affection. The therapist should assess beliefs about how often the couple should act according to the above standards, whether he/she is satisfied with how the standards are being met in the relationship, and how upset he/she becomes when the standards are not met.

Dattilio (2002) proposed that in the case of a parent–child relationship assessment should include parents' beliefs concerning: ruination (i.e. substance misuse will ruin his/her life, or cause harm to the family); perfectionism (the child should behave in a perfect manner); approval/love; obedience (teenagers should never challenge parental rules or opinions); self-blame (a child's misbehaviour is due to poor parenting); and malicious intent (the child's misbehaviour is intended to upset or punish the parents). The child's beliefs should also be assessed regarding the following themes: ruination (parental restrictions will ruin the child's life); autonomy (teenagers should have as much freedom as they want); approval/love (loving parents should always approve child's behaviour); and unfairness (parents should never treat their children in ways that teenagers consider unfair). Assessment should also include family members' global perceptions of family characteristics such as cohesion, problem solving, communication quality, role clarity, emotional expression and values.

The therapist explores (using Socratic questioning) the chain of thoughts that intervene between events in the relationship and each partner's emotional and behavioural responses. During sessions the therapist can look for behavioural cues of individuals' emotional responses and gather information about cognitions. He can interrupt them in order to inquire further about the emotions and any associated cognitions. Family members can be asked to keep daily thought records about distressing events between sessions. The information can be used in functional analysis of specific examples. Family members might possess constructive skills which may be present in certain conditions and as a result negative behaviours are less likely to occur under such conditions. It is important to establish the degree to which the negative interactions have generalized over time and settings.

### *Intervention*

#### *With couples*

In the cognitive approach the couple explore their basic beliefs, then collaboratively redefine key principles and finally restructure their belief system. The restructuring process should be done with each person in the presence of their partner. The therapist must focus equally on each partner's expectations about the nature of an intimate relationship in general and more specifically about their relationship. The couple learn to recognize and identify distortions promptly. Mind reading is a very common distortion which affects relationships. During the week, each partner keeps a log of negative thoughts about his or her partner and labels any distortions in such thoughts (for common distortions see Chapter 2). This logbook should be reviewed by the individual and the therapist in the presence of the partner until the individual can do this exercise successfully. When the couple learn to assign a label to their cognitive distortions, then they are able to re-evaluate the structure of their thinking.

The next step is to help partners to link automatic thoughts with emotions. A useful exercise is to review their logbooks and indicate the links between thought and emotion. In this way spouses accept responsibility about how they feel.

The process of restructuring automatic thoughts involves examining them as hypotheses, gathering evidence to challenge them, considering alternative explanations and testing the predictions. For example, early complaints of couples include particular characteristics of their partners that are the inverse, negative side of those characteristics that once attracted them to their partner. Examining this complaint as a hypothesis gives individuals some hope, and encourages them to investigate further their distortions, and to change their perceptions by questioning and weighing up the evidence for their thinking.

Another important step in the restructuring process involves helping both partners to accept responsibility for the distress in the relationship. This requires evaluation of each partner's attributions regarding the cause of the relationship problems, and realization that the conflicts could be resolved only by working together as a team.

Imagery and/or role-play techniques may be extremely helpful in investigating memories of conflict and emotionally charged situations, in reviving old affection towards each other and in realizing that such feelings can be regenerated by their efforts in working on the relationship. Role-play techniques are also used to bring to the surface feelings or thoughts in couples who are noncommunicative in therapy or treatment sessions.

### *With families*

The focus of therapy with families is twofold: (a) to express family members' expectations of one another and explore how they affect multiple interactions within the family context; and (b) it considers the impact that all of this has on the family's ability to cope with crises, change and other unexpected life events.

Individual family members maintain beliefs about every other member of the family unit, in addition to beliefs about family interaction in general. Emphasis is placed on encouraging family members to become conscientious observers of their own interpretations and evaluations of family interactions. The therapist encourages each member to test the validity of his/her attributions, expectancies about their relationships and about what each perceives regarding the other's actions.

For more detailed cover of how to work with couples and families see Dattilio (2002).

## Elective topic 7: Compliance with treatment

### *Introduction*

Compliance refers to the extent to which the client makes best use of all the elements of the treatment package. This includes pharmacological and nonpharmacological aspects of treatment. In the case of opioid substitution treatment for example, methadone is taken once daily by mouth and in most cases satisfactory relief of withdrawal symptoms is obtained, but if it is not taken daily, or taken in variable amounts, less than optimal control of withdrawal symptoms will be achieved. This may result in an increased risk of heroin use, so clients should be encouraged to take the prescribed dose and request higher doses if necessary. Clients can be reluctant to use methadone optimally due to a number of false beliefs, and may be reluctant to access other interventions offered by the team. They may not be making use of practical nonpharmacological strategies of addressing psychological or social difficulties.

### *Example*

- 'Methadone gets into your bones' – no evidence, or 'Methadone rots your teeth' – prevented by good general dental hygiene.
- 'Methadone is difficult to detoxify from' – this is not the current aim of treatment, once a client has truly stopped using heroin, effective detoxification strategies can be devised. It is self-defeating to continue using heroin due to suboptimal use of methadone, out of a desire to detoxify in the future.

- 'Lower doses of methadone may be better regarded by others, for example childcare authorities or family' – what is usually important for such significant others is achieving stability not the dose of methadone per se.
- 'They are only interested in dishing out methadone' – most teams offer a range of other interventions.
- 'It's not worth finding out about education initiatives, no one would want to employ me afterwards' – there may be specific programmes available.

### *Cognitive-behavioural model of treatment compliance*

Compliance with treatment is a common problem across diagnoses and treatment interventions. One of the cornerstones of cognitive-behavioural therapy is the collaborative approach. This is an extremely important advantage when using CBT with clients presenting with a substance misuse problem. Such clients have typically experienced social stigma and judgemental behaviour from society and professionals. They may have a misguided understanding of treatment facilities, opportunities or availability, which can be due to reluctance to enquire openly and ask for help. Reluctance can be associated with a number of issues which include the following: the illicit status of certain substances; issues of confidentiality; access to medical records by insurance or other companies; lack of information available and incorrect or out-of-date information given by health professionals. In addition to the above, adverse experience with prior treatments or relapse, which may contradict client's and family's expectations about treatment, and predispose to a nihilistic or irresponsible approach to treatment. A CBT approach with the use of Socratic questioning and active collaboration can provide a corrective treatment experience.

### *Assessment and formulation*

The therapist can explore the above issues during assessment, or later on during treatment (when poor compliance is manifested). Exploration of treatment expectations, meaning attributed to treatment, personal responsibility and collaborative therapeutic relationship are typical aspects of the assessment process.

Lateness and nonattendance are common problems in chaotic substance misusers, which can impede the progress of treatment if not managed. The therapist should discuss 'ground rules' with the client at the beginning of the treatment which should include:

- The importance of regular attendance.
- Being on time for sessions.
- Telephoning in advance if the client cannot attend and rescheduling appointments.
- Providing the client with an appointment card, telephone numbers and so on.

Despite this, some clients will turn up late, fail to attend and notify and reschedule appointments. This may be particularly common in the early stages of treatment when clients are still ambivalent about treatment, so the therapist should explore the reasons for lateness and/or nonattendance.

Common reasons for lateness and/or nonattendance are:

- Practical issues, for example childcare while attending sessions or difficulty getting to the centre. The therapist should work with the client using problem-solving techniques.
- Ambivalence about treatment.

The therapist may need to use motivational techniques and explore the client's ambivalent feelings about treatment and reasons for resistance which may be for a number of reasons which clients see as major obstacles such as:

- Previous treatment failure experience
- Multiple relapses
- Unable to cope in certain situations without using
- Stressful home/family/relationship situation
- Impossible to change lifestyle
- Frequent exposure to stimulus conditions.

Arriving intoxicated should be discussed in the 'ground rules' at the outset of treatment. Generally the session should be cancelled and rescheduled, and the therapist should ensure that the client arrives home safely. However, arriving intoxicated may be a sign that the client has experienced a crisis, so even if it is not explored at the time, it should be explored in the next scheduled session.

Other common problems or behaviours suggesting poor compliance include inability to keep other appointments, not taking medication appropriately, not asking for changes if necessary and not disclosing relapse and other problems.

The meaning of any of the above problems should be assessed, discussed openly in a friendly and supportive manner, and ways to resolve them should be agreed collaboratively. Compliance problems should be included in case formulation and if factors affecting compliance are related to other problems such as anxiety, low mood, low self-esteem, these problems and their management should also be included in the formulation and treatment plan.

### *Intervention*

The use of simple language, examples and metaphors and treatment hypothesis that need to be tested, can empower self-control and responsibility. It is helpful to keep clear and simple notes of what has been agreed either by the client or by the therapist using a language easily understood by the client. The agreement should be reviewed and conditions should be adhered to by all sides. The principles of contingency management and motivational interviewing techniques are extremely helpful and should be followed.



## Elective topic 8: Risk behaviours/injecting behaviours

### *Introduction*

Many substance misusers engage in high-risk behaviours which make them vulnerable to HIV, Hepatitis B and C, accidental overdose and other health-related problems. Risk behaviours include sharing drug use equipment such as needles and syringes; this is a particular problem with opiate users who inject. High-risk sexual behaviours are also common in drug users, particularly those for whom prostitution is a financial resource, as well as young people who misuse alcohol. Risk behaviours may need to be addressed early in treatment.

### *Assessment and formulation*

A detailed assessment of risk behaviours is extremely important. The assessment should include behaviours considered risky by: (i) the client; and (ii) significant others. The client's understanding of what constitutes risk behaviour and the reasons why others consider some of his/her behaviours risky should be included. Some clients may not be aware that some of the behaviours they engage in are health risks.

The assessment should include all risk-taking behaviours, should focus on details and should be personal. It should follow the motivational interviewing principles outlined in Chapter 3 and Chapter 6, and should not be judgemental or overdidactic. Information elicited during the assessment should inform the formulation, and on the other hand information already available from formulation should be used to clarify the meaning attributed to practising risk behaviours. For example, injecting might be considered the most glorifying drug-taking method. Mixing certain types of substances might be fashionable within certain group of individuals. The meaning that the client attributes to this behaviour, and the modification of this meaning, are far more important and influential on a successful attempt to change this behaviour, than the actual realistic risk of the behaviour. Information regarding risk can often be ignored (selective attention), and/or the client can be habituated to generic risk messages that he/she considers not to apply to him/her.

### *Intervention*

Like any other behavioural problem, the first step is to prioritize the risk-taking behaviours according to the associated risk, and the client's ability to modify them. Two separate lists should be developed. There may well be a conflict of interests between the two lists. The client and therapist should agree on what behaviours should be targeted first, and the goals for change should be established. The therapist should then help the client to set appropriate realistic goals for starting to change risk-taking behaviours.

The second step is to identify possible barriers to achieving change in risky behaviours. The therapist should enable the client to apply and practise problem-solving and assertiveness skills to overcome such barriers, for example practising assertiveness in negotiating condom use with partner.

Sometimes clients are aware of risk-taking behaviours that need to be modified, but find it difficult not to engage or are ambivalent about the real risk associated with them. Cognitive techniques such as advantages/disadvantages analysis and rational–emotional role-play (as presented in the section 'Elective topic 1') can be helpful.

The therapist should remember the basic rule applicable to all habitual behaviours: (a) specific strategic steps; (b) goals and plans have to be developed, monitored and re-enforced regularly; and (c) practise between sessions is very important.

The therapist should offer specific information/leaflets about risk reduction in relevant areas. These should include: clarification of the concept of harm reduction versus abstinence; methods of transmission of HIV, Hepatitis and other sexually transmitted diseases; risks associated with sharing injection–drug equipment; syringe and needle exchange centre; and use of and how to obtain condoms. The therapist should aim to discuss this information, question the interpretation of the client within the session and use any possible information to re-enforce change.

## Elective topic 9: Repeated criminal behaviour

### *Introduction*

Criminal behaviour is a common problem among substance misusers, however, it may not be a straightforward matter of stealing or shoplifting to fund the drug habit. In several countries, specific treatment programmes have been developed for clients involved with the criminal justice system. These programmes have the dual aim of reducing offending behaviour and treating substance misuse.

### *Assessment and formulation*

Criminal behaviour is not always associated with generating income to obtain substances. It could be the result of intoxication, or substance use might be necessary to reduce performance anxiety. There is a number of issues surrounding repeated criminal behaviour which should be explored. Detailed description of the behaviour and functional analysis although at times problematic (due to illegal and other issues) is important:

- The meaning of the behaviour should be explored and be included in the formulation. Criminal behaviour could be a source of immediate gratification. Compulsive criminal behaviour might be associated with anxiety reduction, or it may be part of a self-destructive attitude towards life. It could also be a source of testing other people's interest (anticipating punishment), and reflect schemata about self-value, life in general and the future.

- Criminal behaviour can become an automatized behaviour which is repeated without any conscious motive. Such behaviours are usually preceded by thoughts and emotions for which the only outlet is to perform the criminal act. These clients are ashamed and embarrassed about their problem.
- A detailed assessment of the behaviours and skills involved might prove beneficial in improving self-esteem and promote overall lifestyle changes. Sometimes drug misusers think that they don't have any skills, and fail to recognize that they have got skills, but they have been developed and used entirely around criminal behaviour. A lack of recognizable skills contributes to low self-esteem and pessimism about the ability to change and develop a new lifestyle.

### *Intervention*

Treatment should follow the steps outlined in the previous topic. In addition, as with the treatment of any other compulsive behaviour, exposure and response prevention can be beneficial. This can be done in the session using imagery, and outside of the session using behavioural experiments (e.g. *in vivo* practice). In *in vivo* exposure, it is essential for the client to be accompanied by a trusted person, and to expose him/herself for enough time to experience all emotions and thoughts. The 'daily thought record' is useful for reducing the automatic nature of the behaviour and to increase control.

Skills involved in criminal behaviour may be transferred and used in the development of more adaptive behaviours. For example, shoplifting involves several skills, such as observation, concentration, movement coordination, control of unpleasant emotions such as anxiety; and social skills, such as pleasant interaction and conversational skills.

It is of paramount importance to help the clients to identify the skills they have got, and to explore ways of using them in creating a new lifestyle.

## Elective topic 10: Sleep management

### *Introduction*

Clients in treatment for a substance misuse problem commonly complain of sleep problems. Complaints may be of reduced quantity of sleep or poor quality of sleep. Difficulty in sleeping may be associated with chronic dysphoria, perceived as an obstacle to further progress in treatment or linked to ongoing use of stimulants or alcohol, or licit or illicit benzodiazepines. In the general population causes of insomnia include:

- Psychiatric disorder (e.g. anxiety and depression) and drugs used in treatment of these.
- Fear of sleeplessness (psycho-physiological insomnia).
- Substance misuse.

- Sleep apnoea.
- Disordered sleep–wake cycle, for example due to shift work.
- Other medical disorders.

Psycho-physiological insomnia is characterized by the complaint of difficulty in sleeping causing reduced performance when awake, trying too hard to get to sleep, increased physical tension, prolonged time trying to get to sleep and frequent wakening during the night.

### *Assessment and formulation*

This should consider the conditions listed below:

- Client's description of onset, lengthened quantity of sleep, daytime drowsiness or reduced performance.
- Descriptions of the above by partner/spouse/relative.
- General medical problems.
- Depressive illness, anxiety disorders.
- Current prescribed drug details (other than methadone).
- Drug and alcohol use.
- Review of withdrawal symptoms.
- Details of sleep environment and hygiene.
- Current circumstances and stresses.

Assessment should also include the client's understanding of good or normal sleep quantity and pattern. Frequently, clients have unrealistic expectations about normality and therefore treatment.

### *Intervention*

A person with a longstanding history of substance misuse is likely to have longstanding sleep abnormalities which may take many months to improve following stabilization of drug use, or later following withdrawal. They should be encouraged to take steps to promote a healthier and more satisfactory sleep pattern, but not to expect dramatic short-term improvement. Sleep problems can be exacerbated by withdrawal from/dose reduction in cannabis, alcohol, benzodiazepines and opiates. Further education on the effect of substance on sleep is appropriate. Table 7.1 might be useful:

**Table 7.1.** Effects of substances on sleep

| Substance | Effect |
|---|---|
| Alcohol | Small amounts act as hypnotic and promote sleep<br>Larger amounts result in rebound and withdrawal effects later in the night, which may prompt wakening |
| Nicotine | Sleep can be disrupted by smoking in the late evening, and during nicotine withdrawal |
| Caffeine | Increased awakenings<br>Sleep disrupted during withdrawal. (Reduced REM sleep) |
| Cannabis | Reduced REM sleep<br>Regular use associated with excessive sleeping and lethargy<br>Sleep disturbance on withdrawal |
| Opiates | Short term effect of promoting sleep<br>Sleep disturbance on withdrawal<br>Long-lasting sleep disturbance can occur even after withdrawal, following long-term opiate dependence |
| Cocaine/amphetamine | Reduce total sleep quantity<br>Excessive sleeping on withdrawal |
| Hallucinogens | No direct effect; sleep may be disrupted by a bad trip |
| Benzodiazepines | Short term hypnotic effect<br>Long term may become ineffective, or contribute to sleep problems |

Therapist should encourage and monitor changes that promote good sleep. These changes include:

1. Application of relaxation techniques.
2. Use of aromatherapy if available.
3. Sleep hygiene advice:
   - education about likely causes of difficulty with sleeping which can include personalized information on client's drug use and sleep difficulties
   - advice to avoid caffeine (coffee or tea) especially late in day
   - optimize bedroom temperature (room temperature should not be too hot.)
   - encourage a regular bed routine, which should include hot bath and hot drink (milk or chamomile tea) before sleep

- exercise in late afternoon or early evening, and not later than at least a few hours before bed time
- small food intake in the evening.

4. Review of substitute dose (*in the case of opioid dependence*): the dose may need to be increased if sleeplessness correlates with a 24-hour cycle of opioid withdrawal symptoms. A detailed assessment of sleep–wake pattern, time of medication intake and sleeplessness-related symptoms is important.

CHAPTER EIGHT

# Therapist training and supervision

## Introduction

All practitioners of any psychological therapy need to be both properly trained in the particular approach and techniques they are using (in this case CBT), and whatever their level of experience, they need to be supervised. Supervision ('the monitoring of practice'; Lewis, 2005) can be taken to vary from managerial monitoring of caseloads, through to therapy for the therapist. Likewise training can vary in meaning from simple attendance at a one-day event to assessment of competencies required for accreditation as a therapist. This chapter aims to describe pragmatic levels expected to fulfil clinical governance in health and social care settings. As with all manual-guided therapies, the specifications given in earlier chapters are intended to standardize therapist technique in order to ensure 'quality assurance', but training and supervision need to go beyond how well the individual components are delivered.

As a minimum, it is essential that the manual-guided sessions are implemented by qualified drug and alcohol workers who are trained to perform them effectively. This means:

- experienced alcohol and drug workers committed to the type of therapy they will be performing;
- training to help therapists challenge their repertoire to meet manual guidelines; and
- ongoing monitoring and supervision of the delivery of treatment.

## Training

Training requirements for developing competency in CBT are not set by any statutory regulating body although organizations such as the British Association for Behavioural and Cognitive Psychotherapies (BABCP), British Association for Counselling and Psychotherapy, United Kingdom Council for Psychotherapy and so on have criteria for accreditation as a CBT therapist within their organizations. In addition, DANOS (Drug and Alcohol National Occupational Standards) gives competency standards that include the delivery of psychological therapies. CBT training courses accredited for example by BABCP tend to be at Diploma level, last for at least one year and include supervised practice (see BABCP web site for details of CBT training courses in the UK). The basic requirements to become accredited with, for example, BABCP are relatively stringent (see BABCP web site) and go beyond completing an accredited course. Simply to deliver the CBT techniques described in this book, whilst less strict than needed for accreditation as a CBT therapist, nevertheless requires a minimum level of competencies and conditions. An example of such is found in the UKCBT Methadone Maintenance Trial (UKCBTMM Project Group, 2004). The basics required for this included having at least one year of clinical experience working with substance misusers. In practice most therapists had a relevant professional training to degree level or equivalent, and this is probably a basic requirement to ensure professional standards are adhered to.

In addition, the therapists in this research trial underwent an intensive two-week (10 working days) programme of training before the intervention phase of the trial. This was run as two separate week-long training sessions, a period of one month apart, during which time the trainees were expected to practise their skills with test cases from their service/clinic. Supervised practice was viewed as an important part of training, and clearly requires a supervisor trained in this therapy. The training programme included instruction on the principles of CBT, its application to addiction, and clinical practice. Methods used included didactic training, role-play, case simulation, scenarios for discussion and video examples. The programme included an overview of the process of therapy outlining the main techniques and their order of application, methods of engaging clients, developing case formulations, using cognitive and behavioural techniques, role-plays and techniques to effect progress in therapy. The subsequent supervision sessions aimed to consolidate and aid the application of knowledge to the therapeutic setting. This training for the research trial probably forms a minimum standard for providing the techniques described in this book.

In addition to training in the CBT techniques, a number of nonspecific factors is also important (see Wanigaratne *et al.*, 2005). There is a growing body of research suggesting that nonspecific factors make a significant contribution to the effectiveness of psychological treatments, including CBT. Client, therapist and process variables may all contribute to the outcome – who attends treatment, who delivers it and how it is delivered may be as important as the actual therapy. There is considerable evidence to show the importance of empathy, warmth and genuineness – seen as the core conditions for psychological therapy – as reviewed for example by Truax and Carkhuff (1967). More recently, other therapist factors have been identified as influencing the effectiveness of treatment (described in Wanigaratne *et al.*, 2005). Therapist factors that contribute to good outcomes for clients include:

- Being empathic and authoritative (Truax and Carkhuff, 1967)
- Being willing to participate in supervision (Luborsky, McLellan and Woody, 1985)
- Using motivational dialogue (Raistrick and Tober, 2004)
- Taking a nonblaming, nonjudgemental stance (Stanton and Shadish, 1997)

- Being a good listener (Truax and Carkhuff, 1967)
- Being in good psychological health (Truax and Carkhuff, 1967)
- Developing a helping alliance: a collaborative relationship between client and therapist (Horvath and Luborsky, 1993).

Thus training and ongoing continuous professional development (CPD) is broader than CBT alone. It is also important to remember with this client group throughout therapy that readiness to change predicts a positive therapeutic alliance (Connors *et al.*, 2000). Strong alliances, in turn, have been associated with positive outcomes in patients who are dependent on alcohol (Connors *et al.*,1997), as well as patients involved in methadone maintenance, on such measures as illicit drug use, employment status and psychological functioning. Good motivational interviewing (MI) skills are therefore probably essential as part of the training and CPD requirements for delivering these CBT topics (and it is this combination of MI and CBT that distinguishes CBT with substance misusers from CBT with other client groups). Furthermore, the practitioner's expertise and competence instil confidence in the treatment and strengthen the therapeutic alliance. Emphasis also should be given to the alliance with a social support network, which can be a powerful predictor of whether the patient stays in treatment (Luborsky, 2000).

It is also worth stating here some of the other guiding principles that underpin effective treatment (Raistrick and Tober, 2004), which should be taken account of within training:

- Accessing treatment sooner rather than later improves outcomes.
- We know that shorter and longer treatment work equally to improve abstinence from substance misuse, but to have an effect on levels of dependence longer episodes of treatment, including CBT, are probably needed.
- Clients with complex needs or coexisting mental illness, social breakdown or instability and physical health problems benefit from greater intensity and broader spectrum interventions, not just CBT.

## Supervision

Like any effective treatment, CBT has the capacity to do harm if it is provided inappropriately or inadequately, or if it is delivered in an unethical fashion. CBT can become unsafe if delivered by untrained practitioners, without adequate supervision, in unskilful ways to the wrong clients with the wrong formulation. Unethical practices are a danger whenever a client is made vulnerable such as in an intensive therapeutic relationship. These dangers could include financial and sexual exploitation of clients at one end of the spectrum, to collusive protracted psychotherapeutic relationships that are wasteful of professional resources at the other. Some 'warning signs' of when a therapist and the client need to be concerned include the therapist being defensive, upset or angry in a session, talking frequently and in detail about their personal life, or asking inappropriate questions for example about the client's sex life (discussed in more detail in Choosing Talking Therapies?, Department of Health, 2001). Therapy might even be seen as potentially abusive, for example if hopes of successful outcomes are raised but not achieved, further reinforcing a person's beliefs of being 'unhelpable' or attributing treatment failure to themselves.

Adequate training and supervision help prevent these hazards. Temple and Bowers (1998) suggest that supervision addresses two main areas; firstly the needs of the practitioner and secondly the needs of the client. The functions of supervision fall into these two areas. Lewis (2005) proposes several main functions of supervision, including:

- To encourage and support the therapist.
- To act as an early warning system when the supervisor becomes aware of the risk of bad practice or ethical problems.
- To be a monitor and develop awareness and reflective practice.
- To encourage, facilitate and focus the therapist's continuing professional development and education.
- To provide a supportive environment for the therapist to become aware of and discuss their own cognitive and behavioural processes and their affective responses to clients.

The process of supervision is sometimes seen as an experiential learning activity and probably the best example of this is known as Kolb's learning cycle (Kolb, 1984). In this cycle, a concrete experience is the subject of observation and reflection in supervision, resulting in a formulation of the experience in terms of abstract concepts and generalizations. This leads to testing the implications of the concepts in new situations which itself becomes a concrete experience and so on in a cycle. The aim of this process is to integrate the learning into the therapist's practice thus building the therapist's competencies and enhancing therapy and the experiences of the client. The components of supervision using the Kolb cycle include:

- The client's presenting problems and issues.
- Any effects these have on the therapist and vice versa, as well as considering the quality of the therapist/client relationship.
- A discussion of the case conceptualization and clinical techniques. Included here are the therapist's skills in assessment and formulation, an appropriate treatment plan and CBT model, as well as intervention techniques and evaluation of treatment progress.
- Appropriateness of the therapist's skill and experience for working with each client and the appropriateness for this agency providing this role.

- The impact of the client and/or the nature of this work on the therapist's physical and psychological health. Is the therapist's case load optimal for well being, is the working environment 'fit for purpose' in promoting effective therapy?
- What can or should the therapist learn about their knowledge and skills from their work? Self-appraisal and reflection in supervision should help identify strengths and areas for development in the therapist.
- The context of therapeutic activity and how the different demands of organizations and a client may present dilemmas for a therapist (e.g. where there are child care issues, or the client confiding information likely to affect their treatment outside of the CBT work).
- Ethical and professional issues. Power imbalances, prejudices or cultural or ethnicity differences. Supervision should function either to facilitate resolutions to these issues or find ways of working with them.

The actual style of supervision will vary according to how senior and experienced the therapist and supervisor are. Typically, with less experienced therapists there is likely to be more of a mentor–learner relationship with an emphasis on monitoring/evaluating what is the content and delivery of CBT, advising and instructing in a more 'teaching' style as well as modelling of skills. With more experienced therapists the emphasis may be on reflection of the process and content of therapy, taking a supportive and sharing role and functioning less as an advisor/teacher and more as a facilitator for collaborative problem solving. Elements of all of these will be present regardless of experience.

A further consideration is whether the clinical supervisor is also the managerial line manager, responsible for monitoring performance. There are potential tensions in combining clinical supervision and management roles. Supervisees could potentially feel inhibited in talking freely about clinical aspects of cases out of awareness of the management role of their supervisor. This needs to be recognized and discussed between supervisor and therapist. Where the roles are divided, with separate clinical and service supervision (common where therapists are in multi-professional teams and receive service supervision from multi-professional team managers), or with clinical supervisors outside service and line management arrangements, there are also risks. Clinical supervisors may make recommendations about a case that are inappropriate to the service. Good coordination between clinical supervisor and service supervisor/line manager is necessary to minimize these risks.

### *Rating of therapists*

It can be helpful to have a concrete basis on which to evaluate therapist implementation of CBT. Most supervision will probably rely on the supervisee reporting to the supervisor on the content and other related issues of sessions. Direct or indirect observations and tapes of the therapist in a session should supplement this, however. Audio or video recording of sessions are probably less intrusive than the supervisor sitting in on sessions. One way of then evaluating the observed session is for therapists and supervisors to complete parallel CBT-adherence rating forms after a session is conducted or viewed. They cover a range of key CBT interventions.

### *Therapist checklist*

The CBT Therapist Checklist (Carroll, 1998) asks therapists to rate the CBT strategies and interventions implemented in a given session and how much the intervention is used. The checklist has a variety of purposes:

- To remind the therapist, at each session, of the key active ingredients of CBT.
- To foster greater therapist adherence to the CBT sessions and topics through self-monitoring.
- To organize and provide the basis for supervision, since therapists can readily note and explore with the supervisor the strategies and interventions they have trouble implementing with a given client.
- To generate a useful record of which interventions were or were not delivered to each client in a given session. For example, one can construct a session-by-session map of the order and intensity of CBT interventions introduced to a range of different client types.
- To allow (in either direction) flexibility of intensity and number of supervisor sessions according to the therapist's perception of need.

### *Rating scale*

The supervisor's version of the form, called the CBT Rating Scale (Carroll, 1998), differs from the therapist's version by adding a skilfulness rating for each item. Thus, for each intervention, both quantity and quality are rated. The scale is an essential part of training.

- It provides structured feedback to the therapist and forms the basis of supervision.
- It provides a method of determining whether a therapist in training is ready to be delivering the treatment with greater autonomy.
- When used with ongoing supervision, it enables the supervisor to monitor and correct therapist 'drift' in implementing the treatment.
- For therapists who have trouble adhering adequately to manual guidelines, but are not fully aware of it discrepancies between the therapist scale and the supervisor's checklist is a useful strategy for enhancing adherence.

Not all items on the rating forms are expected to be covered, or covered at a high level, during all sessions, whilst others reflect the essential CBT approach that should be present, at least to a moderate level, in the majority of sessions.

### Specific guidelines on CBT supervision

The level and intensity of ongoing supervision reflects the experience and skill of the therapist as well as the time available for supervision. BABCP guidance suggests a minimum of 1 hour per month for CBT supervision (as quoted in Lewis, 2005). With less experienced therapists it is recommended that individual supervision is provided as a minimum on a fortnightly basis by the supervisor. The supervision is not necessarily one to one; group supervision is an option as is peer group supervision. Face-to-face supervision might be added to by telephone and e-mail supervision. Supervision sessions can be structured around ratings of adherence to CBT and competence in delivering the treatment, with the supervisor noting when the therapist delivered the treatment effectively as well as areas in need of improvement.

Supervisors should also review and evaluate, possibly using the CBT Rating Scale, one or two randomly selected sessions per client.

Supervision sessions themselves should include a general review of the therapist's current cases, discussion of any problems in implementing CBT, and review of recent ratings from the supervisor. The supervisee and supervisor need to establish a minimum for supervision sessions where the supervisor has directly or indirectly observed/listened to a session. Guidance for the frequency of this does not exist, but as a pragmatic suggestion at least annually for all therapists seems a reasonable minimum.

Supervision is most effective under the following circumstances:

- When it is conducted at a consistent place, date and time.
- When the goals of the supervision are clear and both participants' roles are defined.
- When the procedures that will be used for evaluation of the therapist are clear.
- When feedback to the therapist is focused and concrete.

#### Example

'When you debriefed X's last slip, I thought you didn't get enough information for either of you to really understand what was going on. For example, it wasn't clear to me what was going on beforehand, how much she used, where she got the cocaine, and how the episode ended and she got back in control. I think you should be more thorough in doing functional analysis any time there is an episode of use.'

### Peer supervision

The function of this is:

- To provide peer support.
- To present any complex or difficult cases/issues.
- To receive additional supervision from these discussions.
- To gain reassurance about management of cases.

### *Common problems encountered in supervision*

***Therapist style*** Switching from a CBT style to motivational interviewing, which may be necessary at any stage of this programme, is potentially a problem for therapists. This requires practise and supervision in how to use the styles interchangeably and with greatest effect.

***Balance*** The structure of CBT sessions is intended to integrate skills training with effective, supportive therapy that meets the needs of each client as an individual. Therapists new to CBT and motivational interviewing, particularly those less experienced in treating substance abusers or unaccustomed to a high level of structure in treatment, often let sessions become unfocused, without clear goals, and do not make the transitions needed to deliver skills training effectively. Such therapists often wait to introduce skills training until the last few minutes of the session. This results in rushing through important points, failing to use client examples or get client feedback, and neglecting review of the practice exercises. All of these problems give the impression that skills training is not very important.

Other inexperienced therapists allow themselves to become overwhelmed by the constant substance abuse-related crises presented by a client and fail to focus on skills training or use it as an effective strategy to help the client learn to avoid or manage crisis. Falling into a crisis-driven approach tends to increase, rather than decrease, client anxiety and to undermine self-efficacy. On the other hand, maintaining a relatively consistent session routine and balancing the client-driven discussion of current concerns with a focus on skills and strategies is also a means by which the therapist can model effective coping and problem solving.

Conversely, some therapists become overly fixed and inflexible in their application of skills training and adherence to the manual. Anxious to get it right, they present the material in the manual more or less verbatim and fail to adapt it to the specific needs, coping style and readiness of the particular client.

For example, even though skills training requires considerable activity and commitment from the client, some therapists launch into it with clients who are still highly ambivalent or even resistant to treatment. It is important to remind therapists that the manual is not a script but rather a set of guidelines that provides a clear set of goals and overall structure for the treatment, and that it also requires adaptation to the individual case. This often requires considerable familiarity with the didactic material so that therapists can alter the material for each client and present it in a way that sounds fresh and dynamic. Clients should never be aware that the therapist is following a manual.

***Speeding through material*** Many of the skills training concepts, while seeming straightforward and based on common sense, are quite complex, particularly for clients who have cognitive impairment, psychiatric co-morbidity, limited verbal or abstract reasoning skills, or low baseline levels of coping skills. A common error made by many therapists is to fail to check with clients to make sure they understand the material and how it might be applied to their current concerns. When this occurs, it often takes the form of a lecture rather than a dialogue between the client and therapist. Ideally, for each concept presented, therapists should stop and ask clients to provide an example or to describe the idea in their own words. Another common problem is the client forgetting the content of sessions. Often this may be because of poor memory due to cognitive deficits. If so, the sessions need to be pitched at an appropriate level and speed for the client, with repetitions of sessions if necessary. Referral for an assessment of cognitive deficits may be helpful. Sessions may be modified to assist clients with memory problems (see Wilson and Evans, 2000, for an overview of practical management of memory problems).



***Overwhelming the client*** Some therapists try to present to each client all of the coping strategies in the order given in the manual. For many clients, this is overwhelming. Learning and feeling comfortable with one or two coping strategies is preferable to having only a surface understanding of several strategies. Similarly, if too much material is presented, the time available for practise is limited.

A good general tactic is to start by presenting one of the coping strategies the client already uses and is familiar with, and then to introduce one or two more that are consistent with the client's coping style. Also, new coping strategies can be introduced over a few sessions.

***Unclear strategies*** Therapists should attempt to rehearse general coping strategies using specific examples. However, some therapists use the coping strategies during the session but do not effectively communicate the basic underlying strategy. For example, they may effectively apply problem-solving strategies to clients' problems but fail to make the problem-solving steps explicit or ensure that clients understand the concepts. It is essential that therapists use examples to demonstrate the general, underlying strategy but it is equally important that the general strategy be made clear.

***Not providing specific examples*** Just as some therapists do not effectively communicate underlying principles, others fail to bring the coping skills material alive by using specific examples, based on material provided by the client, to illustrate their points. Skilful therapists make the transition from the client's report of current concerns to the skill-focused section of the session by using specific examples.

***Example***

'Earlier, you talked about how hard it was to deal with Joe and his continuing to drink, and today, I thought we would talk about some ways you might be able to effectively say no to him. How does that sound?'

Again, skills training should be presented as a dialogue between the client and therapist, with the therapist attempting to convey the message, 'Here is something I think can help you with what you're struggling with right now'.

***Downplaying practice exercises*** Although most clients do their exercises, and those who practise outside sessions have better outcomes, a number of therapists do not sufficiently attend to practice exercises. This takes the form of a cursory review of completion of tasks in the beginning of sessions. It also leads to rushing through task assignments at the end of sessions, not being creative in task assignments, and letting practices slide if the patient does not do them. Often, this reflects a therapist's low expectations about the client attempting the exercise (and, often, low expectations about the client's progress).

A review of the assignment provides some structure to the first part of the session and sends the message that outside practise is important. Generally, therapists who expect their clients to practise outside of sessions have clients who do so. Also, therapists and clients are by no means limited to the practice described in this book and are encouraged to come up with their own extra-session tasks.

***Abandoning the manual with difficult clients*** Many clients present with a range of complex and severe co-morbid problems. Therapists may become overwhelmed by concurrent problems and drift from use of the manual in an attempt to address all of the client's problems. In such cases, therapists often take a less structured approach rather than the greater structure needed by the client.

Generally, if the client is sufficiently stable for community-based therapy, the treatment described in the manual is adequate, even for disturbed clients. CBT provides short-term therapy that includes the major attributes of an effective approach to alcohol or drug abuse.

- A highly structured approach to treatment.
- Prioritizing of concurrent problems.
- A primary focus on achieving health and other improvements.

# Pay-off or decision-balance matrix

Behaviour:

| Positive consequences | | Negative consequences | |
|---|---|---|---|
| Short term | Long term | Short term | Long term |
| | | | |

# Rational decision-taking chart

Practise monitoring decisions that you face in the course of a day, both large and small, and consider safe and risky alternatives for each

| Decision | Safe alternative | Risky alternative |
|---|---|---|
| | | |

APPENDIX III

# Steps of problem solving

## Steps of problem solving

1. Identify your problems
2. Decide which one to tackle first
3. Decide on your goal and set targets for yourself
4. Work out the steps that are necessary to achieve your targets
5. Work through the steps towards your goal
6. Recognize your achievement. Reward yourself!

APPENDIX IV

# Weekly activity schedule

(adapted from Beck, 1993)

| Fill in time for each day | MONDAY | TUESDAY | WEDNESDAY | THURSDAY | FRIDAY | SATURDAY | SUNDAY |
|---|---|---|---|---|---|---|---|
| MORNING | Get up | | | | | | |
| AFTERNOON | | | | | | | |
| EVENING | Go to bed | | | | | | |

# References

## Select bibliography


Amato, L., Minozzi, S., Davoli, M. *et al.* 2004 Psychosocial combined with agonist maintenance treatments versus agonist maintenance treatments alone for treatment of opioid dependence (Cochrane Review). *The Cochrane Library*. Issue 4. Chichester, UK: John Wiley & Sons, Ltd.

Amato, L., Minozzi, S., Davoli, M. *et al.* (2004) Psychosocial and pharmacological treatments versus pharmacological treatments for opioid detoxification (Cochrane Review). *The Cochrane Library*. Issue 4. Chichester, UK: John Wiley & Sons, Ltd.

Baker, A., Lee, N.K., Claire, M. *et al.* (2005) . Brief cognitive-behavioural interventions for regular amphetamine users: a step in the right direction. *Addiction*, **100** 3, 367–378

Bandura, A. (1977) Self-efficacy: toward a unifying theory of behavioral change. *Psychological Review* **84**, 191–215.

BABCP website: www.babcp.org.uk.

Beck, A.T. (1967) . *Depression: Causes and Treatment.* Philadelphia: University of Pennsylvania Press.

Beck, A.T. (1976) . *Cognitive Therapy and the Emotional Disorders.* New York: International Universities Press.

Beck, J.S. (1995) *Cognitive Therapy: Basics and Beyond.* New York, Guilford Press

Beck, A.T., Emery, G. (1977) . *Cognitive Therapy of Substance Abuse.* Center for Cognitive Therapy, Philadelphia.

Beck, A.T., Wright, F.D., Newman, C.F., Liese, B.S. (1993) . *Cognitive Therapy of Substance Abuse*, Guilford Press, London.

Bennett-Levy, J., Butler, G., Fennell, M., Hackmann, A. (2004) . *Oxford Guide to Behavioural Experiments in Cognitive Therapy*. Oxford University Press, Oxford.

Bien, T.H., Miller, W.R., Tonigan, J.S. (1993) . Brief interventions for alcohol problems: a review. *Addiction*, **88**, 315–336.

Carroll, K.M. (1998) *A Cognitive-Behavioral Approach to Treating Cocaine Addiction.* National Institute on Drug Abuse. Washington, DC, USA: (Publication Number 98-4308) http://www.nida.nih.gov/TXManuals/CBT

Carroll, K., Rounsaville, B., Nich, C. *et al.* (1994) . One year follow-up of psychotherapy and pharmacotherapy for cocaine dependence: delayed emergence of psychotherapy effects. *Archives of General Psychiatry*, **51**, 989–997

Clark, D.M., Hawton, K., Salkovskis, P.M., Kirk, J., Clark, D.M. (1995) . *Cognitive-Behaviour Therapy for Psychiatric Problems: A Practical Guide.* Oxford University Press, Oxford, In 89–96.

Connors, C.J., Carroll, K.M., DiClemente, C.C. *et al.* (1997) . The therapeutic alliance and its relationship to alcoholism treatment participation and outcome. *Journal of Counselling and Clinical Psychology*, **654**, 588–598

Connors, C.J., DiClemente, C.C., Dermen, K.H. *et al.* (2000) Predicting the therapeutic alliance in alcoholism treatment. *Journal of Studies on Alcohol*, **61**, 139–149.

Curran, H.V., Drummond, D.C. (2006) Psychological treatments for substance misuse and dependence. In Nutt, D.J., Robbins, T.W., *Drugs and the Future: Brain Science and Addiction*. Elsevier, London.

Curran, H.V., Collins, R., Fletcher, S. *et al.* (2003) . Older adults and withdrawal from benzodiazepine hypnotics in general practice: effects on cognitive function, sleep, mood and quality of life. *Psychological Medicine* **33**, 1223–1237

Dattilio, F.M. (2002) . Techniques and strategies with couples and families. In Simos, G., *Cognitive-Behaviour Therapy. A Guide for the Practising Clinician*; Brunner-Routlege, 242–274.

Department of Health. (2001) *Choosing Talking Therapies?* Department of Health, London.

*Drug Misuse and Dependence – Guidelines on Clinical Management*. Department of Health, London, (1999).

Drummond, D.C. and Perryman, K.P (2006). Psychosocial interventions in pharmacotherapy of opioid dependence: a literature review. Report to the World Health Organisation.

Eysenck, H.J. (1952) The effects of psychotherapy: an evaluation. *Journal of Consulting Psychology*, **16**, 319–24

Faggiano, F., Vigna-Taglianti, F., Versino, E., Lemma, P. (2003) Methadone maintenance at different dosages for opioid dependence (Cochrane Review). *The Cochrane Library*. Issue 3. Chichester, UK: John Wiley & Sons, Ltd.

Fairburn, C.G., Cooper, Z., Shafran, R. (1998) A cognitive-behavioural theory of anorexia nervosa. *Behaviour Research and Therapy*, **37**, 1–13

Fairburn, C.G., Cooper, Z., Shafran, R. (2003) Cognitive behaviour therapy for eating disorders: a "transdiagnostic" theory and treatment. *Behaviour Research and Therapy*, **41**, 509–528.

Farrell, M., Ward, J., Mattick, R. *et al.* (1994) . Methadone maintenance treatment in opiate dependence: a review. *British Medical Journal*, **309**, 997–1001

Feeney, G., Young, R., Connor, J. *et al.* (2002) Cognitive behaviour therapy combined with the relapse-prevention medication acamprosate: are short-term treatment outcomes for alcohol dependence improved? *The Australian and New Zealand Journal of Psychiatry* **36**, 622–628

Fennell, M.J. (1995) . Depression. In Hawton, K., Salkovskis, P.M., Kirk, J., Clark, D.M., *Cognitive-Behaviour Therapy for Psychiatric Problems: A Practical Guide*; Oxford University Press, 169–234.

Fennell, M.J. (1998) . Low self-esteem. In Tarrier, N., Wells, A., Haddock, G., *Treating Complex Cases. The Cognitive-Behavioural Therapy Approach*. John Wiley & Sons, 217–240.

Green, B.L., Lindy, J.D., Grace, M.C., Leonard, A.C. (1992) Chronic post-traumatic stress disorder and diagnostic co-morbidity in a disaster sample. *Journal of Nervous and Mental Disease*, **180**, 760–766

Greenberger, D., Padesky, C.A. (1995) . *Mind over Mood; Change How You Feel by Changing the Way You Think*. The Guilford Press, New York.

Higgins, S.T., Petry, N.M. (1999) . Contingency management incentives for sobriety. *Alcohol Research and Health*, **232**, 122–127

Higgins, S.T., Budney, A.J., Bickel, W.K. *et al.* (1993) Achieving cocaine abstinence with a behavioral approach. *American Journal of Psychiatry*, **150**, 763–769

Higgins, S.T., Budney, A.J., Bickel, W.K. *et al.* (1994) . In centives improve outcome in outpatient behavioral treatment of cocaine dependence. *Archives of General Psychiatry*, **51**, 568–576

Horvath, A.O., Luborsky, L. (1993) The role of the therapeutic alliance in psychotherapy. *Journal of Consulting and Clinical Pychology*, **64**, 561–573

Howells, K. (1998) . Cognitive behavioural interventions for anger, aggression and violence. In Tarrier, N., Wells, A., Haddock, G., *Treating Complex Cases. The Cognitive-Behavioural Therapy Approach*. John Wiley & Sons, 295–318.

Hubbard, R.L., Marsden, M.E., Rachal, J.V. *et al.* (1989) . *Drug Abuse Treatment: A National Study of Effectiveness*. Chapel Hill: University of North Carolina Press.

Iguchi, M.Y., Belding, M.A., Morral, A.R. *et al.* (1997) Reinforcing operants other than abstinence in drug abuse treatment: an effective alternative for reducing drug use. *Journal of Consulting & Clinical Psychology*, **65** 3, 421–428.

Kadden, R.M. *et al.* (1995) *Cognitive-Behavioral Coping Skills Therapy Manual: A Clinical Research Guide for Therapists Treating Individuals with Alcohol Abuse and Dependence.* Vol. 3 NIAAA, Rockville, MD:(Project Match Monograph)

Kimble, M.O., Riggs, D.S., Keane, T.M. (1998) . Cognitive behavioural treatment for complicated cases of post-traumatic stress disorder. In Tarrier, N., Wells, A., Haddock, G., *Treating Complex Cases. The Cognitive-Behavioural Therapy Approach*; John Wiley & Sons, 105–130.

Kolb, D. (1984) *Experiential Learning*. Englewood Cliffs, NJ: Prentice Hall.

Kouimtsidis, C., Reynolds, M., Hunt, M. *et al.* (2003) Substance use in the general hospital. *Addictive Behaviours*, **28**, 483–499.

Kuehlwein, K.T. (2002) . The cognitive treatment of depression. In Simos, G., *Cognitive-Behaviour Therapy. A Guide for the Practising Clinician*; Brunner-Routlege, 3–48.

Lewis, K.May (2005) The supervision of cognitive and behavioural psychotherapists. *BABCP Magazine Supplement*, May Issue.

Lingford-Hughes, A.R., Welch, S., Nutt, D.J. (2004) . Evidence-based guidelines for the pharmacological management of substance misuse, addiction and comorbidity: recommendations from the British Association for Psychopharmacology, *Journal of Psychopharmacology*, **18** 3, 293–335

Luborsky, L. (2000) A pattern-setting therapeutic alliance study revisited: 'helping alliances in psychotherapy'. *Psychotherapy Research*, **10**, 17–29

Luborsky, L., McLellan, A.T., Woody, G.E. (1985) Therapist success and its determinants. *Archives of General Psychiatry*, **42** 6, 602–611

Marlatt, G.A., Gordon, J.R. (1985) . *Relapse Prevention: Maintenance Strategies in the Treatment of Addictive Behaviors*, Guilford Press, London.

Marlatt, G.A., Witkiewitz, K. In Marlatt, G.A., Donovan, D.M., (2005) . *Relapse Prevention: Maintenance Strategies in the Treatment of Addictive Behaviors*; Guilford Press, New York, 1–44.

Marsch, L.A. (1998) . The efficacy of methadone maintenance interventions in reducing illicit opiate use, HIV risk behaviour and criminality: a meta-analysis. *Addiction* **93**, 515–532.

Mayet, S., Farrell, M., Ferri, M. *et al.* (2004) Psychosocial treatment for opiate abuse and dependence. *The Cochrane Database of Systematic Reviews*, 4.10.1002/14651858.CD004330.pub2 Art. No.: CD004330

Miller, W.R., Rollnick, S. (1991) *Motivational Interviewing: Preparing People to Change Addictive Behaviour*, Guilford Press, New York.

Miller, W.R., Rollnick, S. (2002) *Motivational Interviewing: Preparing People for Change Addictive Behaviour*, Guilford Press, New York.

Miller, W.R., Wilbourne, P.D., Hetema, J.E. (2003) . What works? A summary of alcohol treatment outcome research. In Hester, R.K., Miller, W.R., *Handbook of Alcoholism Treatment Approaches: Effective Alternatives*, 3rd edn, Boston, MA: Allyn and Bacon. 13–63.

Minozzi, S., Amato, L., Vecchi, S. *et al.* (2006) Oral naltrexone maintenance treatment for opioid dependence (Cochrane Review). *The Cochrane Library*. Issue 1. Chichester, UK: John Wiley & Sons, Ltd.

*Models of Care for the Treatment of Drug Misusers: Part 2*. National Treatment Agency for Substance Misuse, Department of Health, London, 74–78. (2002)

Monti, P.M., Abrams, D.B., Kadden, R.M., Cooney, N.L. (1989) *Treating Alcohol Dependence: A Coping Skills Training Guide*, Guilford Press, London.

Moncrieff, J., Drummond, D.C., Candy, B. *et al.* (1996) Sexual abuse in people with alcohol problems: a study of the prevalence of sexual abuse and its relationship to drinking behaviour. *British Journal of Psychiatry*, **169** 3, 355–360.

Mowrer, O.H. (1960) . *Learning Theory and Behaviour*. Wiley, New York

Newman, M.G., Borkovec, T.D. (2002) Cognitive behavioural therapy for worry and generalised anxiety disorder. In Simos, G., *Cognitive-Behaviour Therapy. A Guide for the Practising Clinician*; Brunner-Routledge, 150–172.

Niaura, R.S. (2000) Cognitive social learning and related perspectives on drug craving. *Addiction* **95** Suppl. S155–S163

Norton, R.N., Morgan, M.Y. (1989) The role of alcohol in mortality and morbidity from interpersonal violence. *Alcohol and Alcoholism*, **24** 6, 565–576

O'Malley, S.S., Jaffe, A.J., Chang, G. *et al.* (1992) Naltrexone and coping skills therapy for alcohol dependence. *Archives of General Psychiatry* **49**: 881–887.

Otto, M.W., Pollack, M.H., Sachs, G.S. *et al.* (1993) . Discontinuation of benzodiazepine treatment: efficacy of cognitive-behavioral therapy. *American Journal of Psychiatry*, **150** 10, 1485–1490

Ouimette, P.C., Moos, R.H., Finney, J.W. (2000) Two-year mental health service use and course of remission in patients with substance use and post-traumatic stress disorders. *Journal of Studies on Alcohol*, **61**, 247–253.

Petry, N.M., Martin, B., Cooney, J.L., Kranzler, H.R. (2000) . Give them prizes, and they will come: contingency management for treatment of alcohol dependence. *Journal of Consulting and Clinical Psychology*, **68** 2, 250–257.

Preston, K.L., Umbricht, A., Wong, C.J., Epstein, D.H. (2001) . Shaping cocaine abstinence by successive approximation. *Journal of Consulting and Clinical Psychology*, **69**, 643–654

Prochaska, J.O., DiClemente, C.C. (1992) Stages of change in the modification of problem behaviours. *Progress in Behavior Modification*, **28**, 184–218

Raistrick, D., Tober, G. (2004) Psychosocial interventions. *Psychiatry*, **3**, 36–39

Raistrick, D., Heather, H., Godfrey, C. (2006) *Review of the Effectiveness of Treatment for Alcohol Problems.* London: National Treatment Agency for Substance Misuse, Department of Health.

Rawson, R.A., Huber, A., McCann, M. *et al.* (2002) A comparison of contingency management and cognitive-behavioral approaches during methadone maintenance treatment for cocaine dependence. *Archives of General Psychiatry* **59**, 817–824

Recommendations for the appropriate use of opioids for persistent non-cancer pain A consensus statement prepared on behalf of the Pain Society, the Royal College of Anaesthetists, The Royal College of General Practitioners and the Royal College of Psychiatrists (March 2004) www.britishpainsociety.org/pdf/opioids_doc_2004.pdf (accessed February 2005).

Reynolds, M., Mezey, G., Chapman, M. *et al.* (2005) . Co-morbid post-traumatic stress disorder in a substance misusing clinical population. *Drugs and Alcohol Dependence*, **77**, 251–58

Reynolds, M., Kouimtsidis, C., Kharla, S. *et al.* (2006). *Co-morbid post-traumatic stress disorder in a substance misusing clinical population: a community sample (personal communication).*

Roozen, H., Boulogne, J., Tulder, M. *et al.* (2004) A systematic review of the effectiveness of the community reinforcement approach in alcohol, cocaine and opioid addiction. *Drug Alcohol Depend* **74**, 1–13.

Salkovskis, P.M. In Hawton, K., Salkovskis, P.M., Kirk, J., Clark, D.M., (1995) . *Cognitive-Behaviour Therapy for Psychiatric Problems: A Practical Guide*; Oxford University Press, 235–276.

Stanton, M.D., Shadish, W.R. (1997) Outcome, attrition, and family-couples treatment for drug abuse: a meta-analysis and review of the controlled, comparative studies. *Psychological Bulletin*, **122** 2, 170–191

Stotts, A.L., Schmitz, J.M., Rhoades, H.M., Grabowski, J. (2001) . Motivational interviewing with cocaine-dependent patients: a pilot study. *Journal of Consulting and Clinical Psychology*, **69**, 858–862

Sue, D., Sue, D.W., Sue, S. (2003) *Understanding Abnormal Behaviour.* 7th edn Houghton Mifflin.

Sutker, P.B., Uddo, M., Brailey, K. *et al.* (1994) Psychological symptoms and psychiatric diagnoses in operation desert storm troops serving graves registration duties. *Journal of Traumatic Stress*, **1**, 159–171.

Temple, S., Bowers, W.A. (1998) Supervising cognitive therapists from diverse fields. *Journal of Cognitive Therapy: An International Quarterly*. **12**, 139–152

Truax, D.B., Carkhuff, R.R. (1967) *Towards Effective Counseling and Psychotherapy*. Chicago: Aldine Publishing Company

UKCBTMM Project Group (2004) *The Effectiveness and Cost Effectiveness of Cognitive-Behaviour Therapy for Opiate Misusers in Methadone Maintenance Treatment: A Multi-Centre, Randomised Controlled Trial*. Department of Health, London

Vorma, H., Naukkarinen, H., Sarna, S., Kuoppasalmi, K. (2002) . Treatment of out-patients with complicated benzodiazepine dependence: comparison of two approaches. *Addiction*, **97** 7, 851–859

Ward, J., Mattick, R., Hall, W. (1997) *Maintenance Treatment and other Opioid Replacement Therapies*. London: Harwood.

Wanigaratne, S., Davis, P., Pryce, K. and Brotchie, J.( (2005) ). *The effectiveness of psychological therapies on drug misusing clients, National Treatment Agency for Substance Misuse*, Research Briefing Paper No. 11.

Weaver, T., Stimson, G., Tyrer, P. *et al.* (2003) Comorbidity of substance misuse and mental illness in community mental health and substance misuse services. *The British Journal of Psychiatry*, **183**, 304–313

Wilson, B., Evans, J.R. (2000) Practical management. In Berrios, G.E., Hodges, J.R., *Memory Disorders in Psychiatric Practice*. Cambridge University Press

Woody, G.E., Luborsky, L., McLellan, A. *et al.* (1983) Psychotherapy for opiate addicts: does it help? *Archives of General Psychiatry*, **40**, 639–645

# Index